crocheted dogs

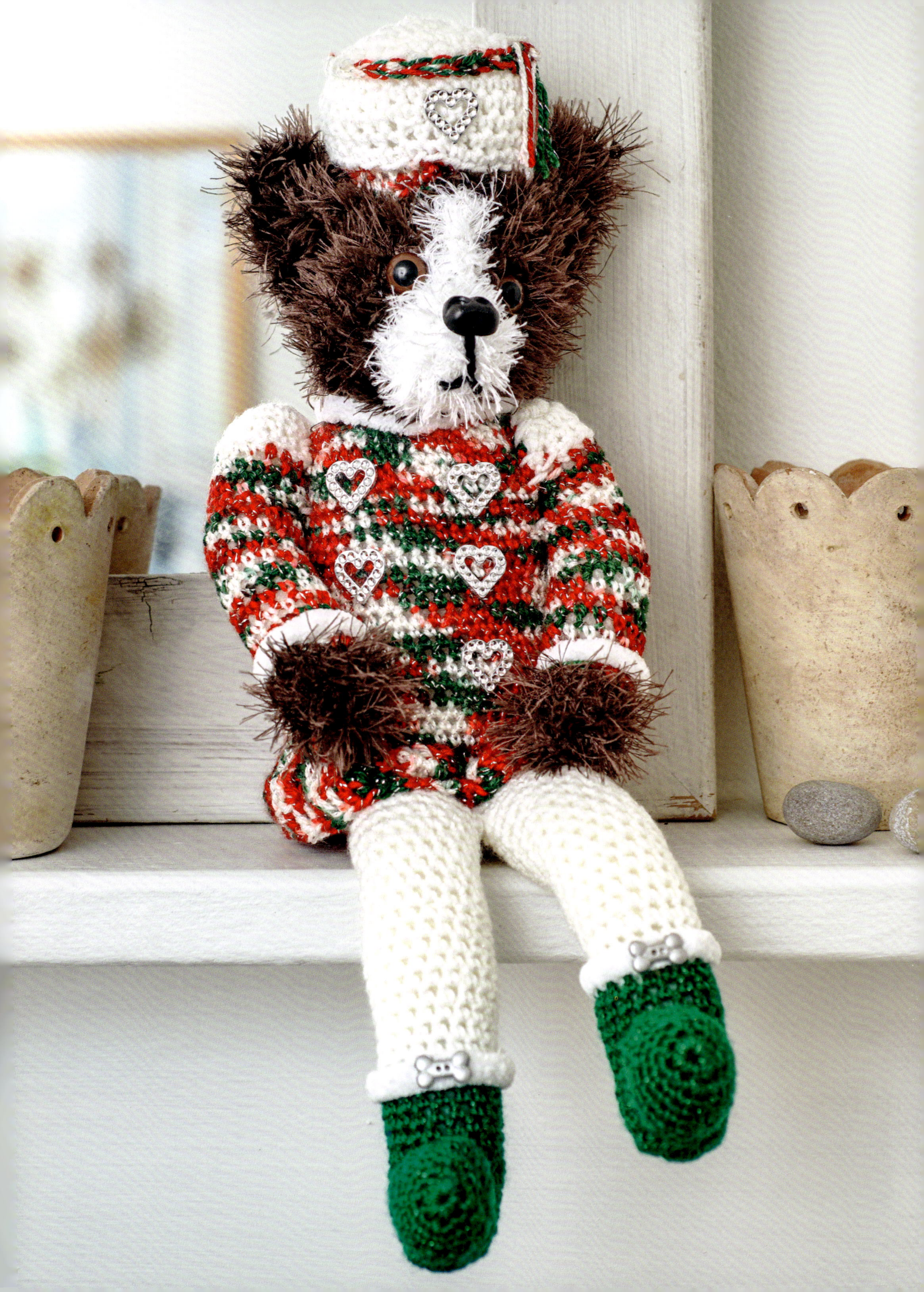

crocheted dogs

CUTE CANINE PATTERNS FOR PILLOWS, BAGS, ACCESSORIES, AND MORE

BARBARA DONOVAN OF JOSEPH BEAR DESIGNS

CICO BOOKS

Dedicated to my beloved Yorkshire Terrier, Tilly, who inspired me to start on my journey of creating crocheted dogs.

Published in 2025 by CICO Books
an imprint of Ryland Peters & Small Ltd
1452 Davis Bugg Road, Warrenton, NC 27589
www.rylandpeters.com

10 9 8 7 6 5 4 3 2 1

Text © Barbara Donovan 2025
Design, illustration, and photography © CICO Books 2025

The designs in this book are copyright and must not be crocheted for sale.

The author's moral rights have been asserted. All rights reserved. No part of this publication may be reproduced, stored in a retrieval system, or transmitted in any form or by any means, electronic, mechanical, photocopying, or otherwise, without the prior permission of the publisher.

US Library of Congress CIP data has been applied for.

ISBN: 978 1 80065 423 5

Printed in China

Editor: Marie Clayton
Pattern checker: Jemima Bicknell
Designer: Alison Fenton
Photographer: James Gardiner
Stylist: Nel Haynes
Illustrator: Stephen Dew

In-house editor: Jenny Dye
Art director: Sally Powell
Creative director: Leslie Harrington
Head of production: Patricia Harrington
Publishing manager: Carmel Edmonds

Note: If you are making a project for a young child or if it will be within reach of a young child, substitute the safety nose and eyes and any embellishments or beads with embroidery in yarn (see page 141).

FSC
MIX
Paper | Supporting responsible forestry
www.fsc.org
FSC® C008047

contents

Introduction 6

CHAPTER 1
pillows 8

Old English Sheepdog Pillow 10
Border Terrier Square Pillow 13
West Highland Terrier Pillow 16
Bearded Collie Pillow 19
Yorkshire Terrier Pillow 22
Fluffy Dog Silhouette Pillows 25
Brown Spaniel Pillow 28
Husky Pillow 31
Border Collie Pillow 34
Bichon Frisé Pillow 37
German Shepherd Pillow 40
Chocolate Labrador Pillow 43
French Bulldog Pillow 46
Poodle Pillow 49

CHAPTER 2
home décor 52

Dachshund Draft Excluder 54
Fluffy Terrier Wall Hanging 59
Doggie Doorstops 62
Fluffy Dog Framed Wall Hanging 66
Small Framed Poodles 69

CHAPTER 3
decorative and cuddly dogs 72

Yorkshire Terrier and Cairn Terrier 74
Chihuahua Nutcracker 79
Spaniel Cuddle Buddy 84
Pomeranian Pumpkin Pal 88
West Highland Terrier Cuddle Pal 92

CHAPTER 4
bags and accessories 96

Shih Tzu Purse 98
Terrier Large Tote Bag 101
Labradoodle Makeup/Clutch Bag 104
Maltese Terrier Purse 107
Cockapoo Purse 110
Poodle Golf Club Covers 113
Chocolate Labrador Makeup Bag and
   Coin Purses 116
Jack Russell Terrier Golf Club Cover 120
Husky Small Shoulder Bag 123
Pug Makeup Bag 126
Schnauzer Purse 129

Techniques 132
Index 143
Suppliers and Acknowledgments 144

introduction

I am delighted to be able to offer my new collection of crocheted dog patterns. I began crocheting many years ago trying to replicate my own dog, Tilly, a Yorkshire Terrier, creating pillows and bags. It was so successful that soon friends were asking me to design and make items similar to their much-loved canine companions.

My love of dogs and crochet has inspired many of my designs over the years and I am pleased to share some of my creations with you. My patterns are aimed at all skill levels so are perfect for beginners through to more experienced crocheters.

With projects of all sizes, this book is divided into four chapters: Pillows, Home Décor, Decorative and Cuddly Dogs, and Bags and Accessories. The patterns enable you to create your own or a loved one's pet just by changing the yarn colors to produce their exact likeness. What great gifts these would be to crochet for friends and family!

Many of the patterns in this book can be adapted to create different projects. You can easily make a pillow into a stylish bag by omitting the pillow form, leaving the top open when you sew the front and back pieces together, and adding plastic, bamboo, or crocheted handles (see page 112). Alternatively, many of the bags can be made into pillows in various sizes by leaving out the handles and inserting a pillow form or toy fiberfill. You could even make a pillow or bag pattern into a pajama case to brighten up any bedroom—simply leave out the handles or pillow form, and sew the front and back pieces together, leaving the top open.

The beauty of these projects is that gauge is not important. I am a very loose crocheter myself, while many people are very tight with their crochet work. Whatever your gauge, you will create a cute and cuddly design.

I hope that you enjoy crocheting these patterns as much as I have enjoyed designing them.

BEFORE YOU BEGIN

If you are new to crochet, all the Techniques you will need are covered on pages 132–141. The Abbreviations used in the crochet patterns are explained on page 142. Each project has a skill rating, from Easy (one circle) to Intermediate (two circles) and Advanced (three circles). Start with the Easy patterns then move on to the next two levels once you know the basic techniques.

introduction 7

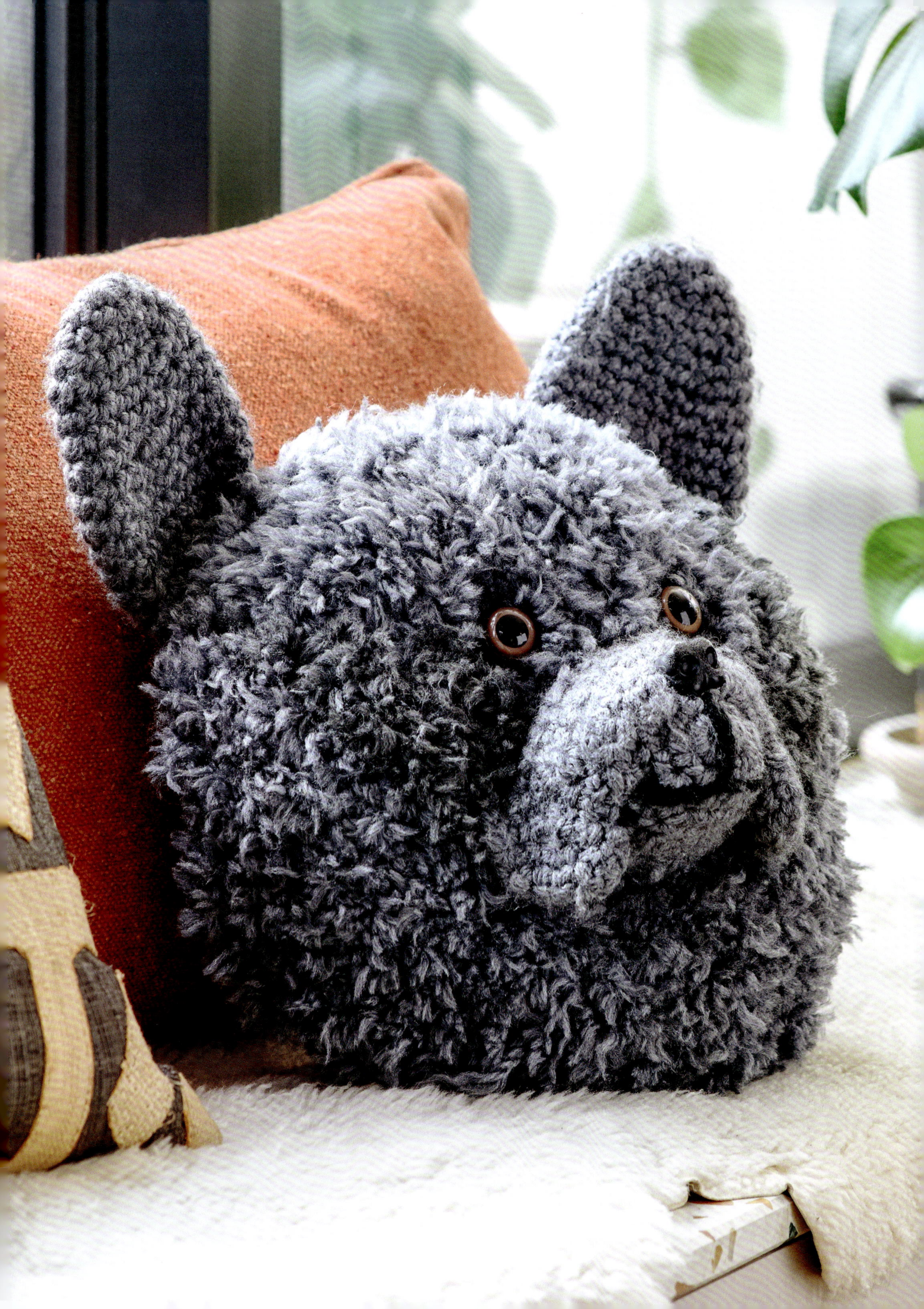

CHAPTER 1
pillows

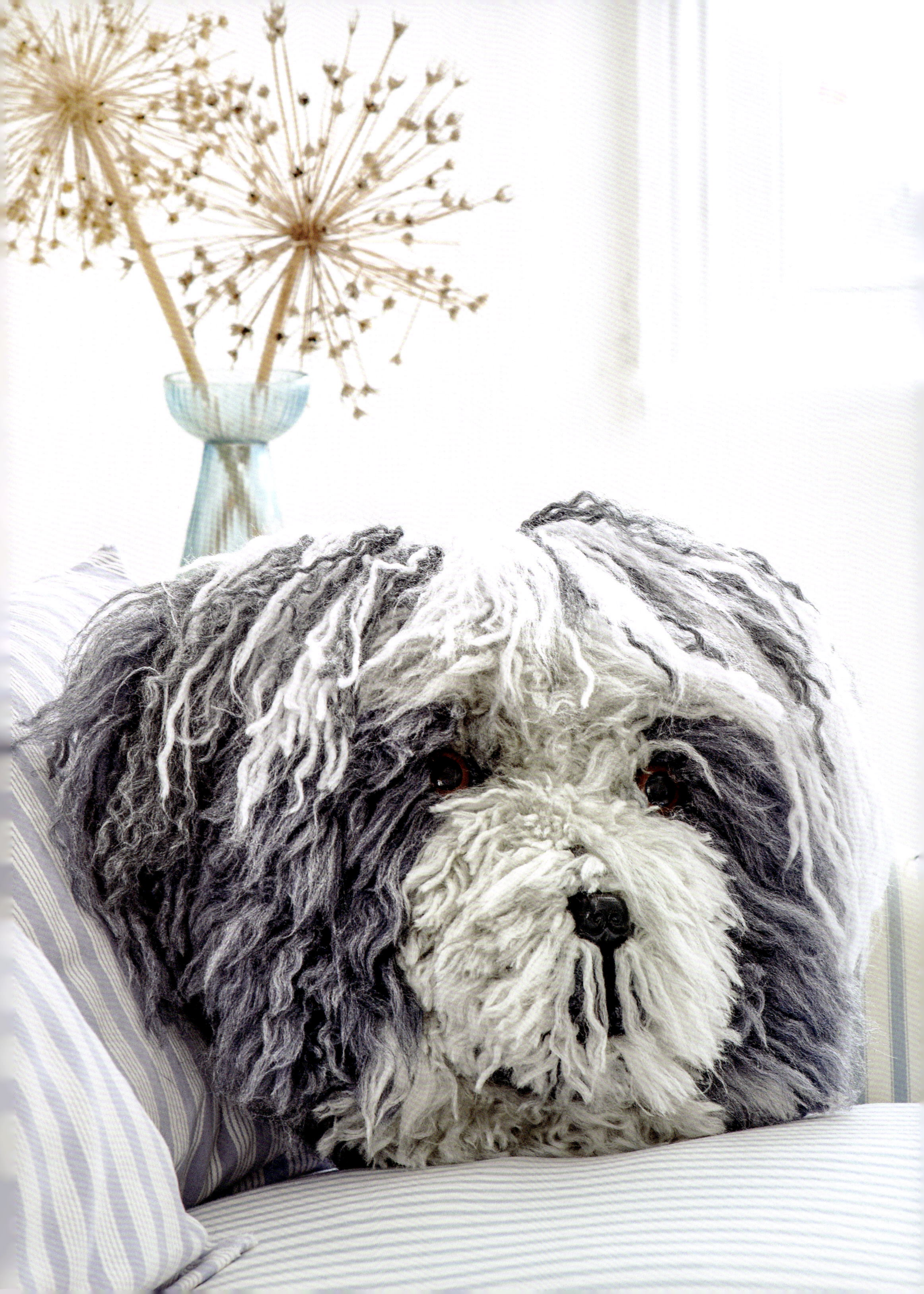

With its fluffy face, this charming sheepdog is a traditional breed that is loved by everyone. The main pillow is made as two pieces of double crochet that are joined together, with the snout worked in single crochet stitch. The soft fur can be added in shades of your choice, then brushed and trimmed to the desired length.

old english sheepdog pillow

SKILL RATING ● ● ○

YARN AND MATERIALS
King Cole Big Value Super Chunky (100% acrylic), super bulky (super chunky) weight yarn, 90yd (81m) per 3½oz (100g) ball
- 3 balls of Graphite 1545 (dark gray) (A)
- 1 ball of White 1758 (B)
- 1 ball of Gray 24 (C)

Small amount of black light worsted (DK) weight yarn (D)

1 3/16in (30mm) safety nose

Small amount of toy fiberfill

Pair of 1in (24mm) safety eyes

14in (35.5cm) diameter pillow form

HOOK AND EQUIPMENT
US J-10 (6mm) crochet hook

Stitch marker

Yarn needle

Stiff brush or pet brush

FINISHED SIZE
Approx. 15in (38cm) diameter

ABBREVIATIONS
See page 142.

PILLOW FRONT AND BACK
(make 2)

Round 1: Using A, ch4, join with a sl st to form a ring.
Round 2: Ch3 (counts as first dc), 11dc in ring, join with a sl st. (*12 sts*)
Round 3: Ch3, 1dc in same dc, [2dc in next dc] to end, join with a sl st. (*24 sts*)
Round 4: Ch3, 2dc in next dc, [1dc in next dc, 2dc in next dc] to end, join with a sl st. (*36 sts*)
Round 5: Ch3, 1dc in next dc, 2dc in next dc, [1dc in each of next 2 dc, 2dc in next dc] to end, join with a sl st. (*48 sts*)
Round 6: Ch3, 1dc in each of next 2 dc, 2dc in next dc, [1dc in each of next 3 dc, 2dc in next dc] to end, join with a sl st. (*60 sts*)
Round 7: Ch3, 1dc in each of next 3 dc, 2dc in next dc, [1dc in each of next 4 dc, 2dc in next dc] to end, join with a sl st. (*72 sts*)
Round 8: Ch3, 1dc in each of next 4 dc, 2dc in next dc, [1dc in each of next 5 dc, 2dc in next dc] to end, join with a sl st. (*84 sts*)
Round 9: Ch3, 1dc in each of next 5 dc, 2dc in next dc, [1dc in each of next 6 dc, 2dc in next dc] to end, join with a sl st. (*96 sts*)
Fasten off.

SNOUT
Round 1: Using A, ch4, join with a sl st to form a ring.
Round 2: Ch1 (counts as first sc), 7sc in ring, join with a sl st. (*8 sts*)
Round 3: Ch1, 1sc in same sc, [2sc in next sc] to end, join with a sl st. (*16 sts*)
Round 4: Ch1, 2sc in next sc, [1sc in next sc, 2sc in next sc] to end, join with a sl st. (*24 sts*)
Rounds 5 and 6: Ch1, 1sc in next sc, 1sc in each sc to end, join with a sl st.
Round 7: Ch1, 1sc in next sc, 2sc in next sc, [1sc in each of next 2 sc, 2sc in next sc] to end, join with a sl st. (*32 sts*)
Rounds 8–12: Ch1, 1sc in next sc, 1sc in each sc to end, join with a sl st.
Fasten off.

TO MAKE UP
Place the front and back with right sides together. Using A, work a single crochet seam (see page 14) around, leaving an opening of approx. 6in (15cm). Turn right side out.

Using D, sew the mouth markings onto the snout (see page 141) using the photo as a guide. Insert the safety nose and secure with the back (see page 141). Stuff the snout firmly and sew to the front of the pillow in the position required.

Add the eyes above the snout and secure with the backs. Insert the pillow form, and then sew the opening closed.

ADDING FUR
Adding the fur on the face can be done in two ways, either with a crochet hook (see page 141) or threading each strand through with a yarn needle and then tying the ends into a knot close to the fabric. The needle is better for getting into small areas, such as around the eyes.

Ears
Cut lengths of A and B approx. 10in (25.5cm) long. Starting from the side of head, add fur fringing in both colors to form the ears for approx. 1in (2.5cm) on either side of the top of the pillow. Brush to give the fluffy effect and trim to length required.

Snout and forehead
Cut lengths of A and C approx. 5in (12.5cm) long. Starting at top of the snout in the center, add a line of fur fringing in the six stitches along the top to the nose on one side. Repeat on other side of the snout. Continue to add fur fringing across forehead, and over and around the snout. Brush for the "fluffy" effect and trim to approx. 1in (2.5cm) long.

Lower face fur
Using 5in (12.5cm) lengths in C, add lines of fur fringing to cover the bottom of the face and under the snout. Brush and trim in line with the bottom of the pillow.

border terrier square pillow

You would think that this happy Border Terrier is sitting next to you with its little face looking so lifelike. This large bright pillow would be perfect for any lounge, sunroom, or bedroom. The pillow is made in double crochet stitch on both sides with the little face worked in single crochet.

SKILL RATING ● ● ○

YARN AND MATERIALS
King Cole Big Value Super Chunky Stormy (100% acrylic), super bulky (super chunky) weight yarn, 90yd (81m) per 3½oz (100g) ball
- 4 balls of Horizon 4108 (orange and light brown) (A)

King Cole Big Value Super Chunky (100% acrylic), super bulky (super chunky) weight yarn, 90yd (81m) per 3½oz (100g) ball
- 1 ball of Latte 3490 (light brown) (B)
- Small amount of Brass 3400 (orange brown) (C)
- ½ ball of Champagne 12 (white) (D)

King Cole Quartz Super Chunky (90% acrylic, 10% wool), super bulky (super chunky) weight yarn, 92yd (85m) per 3½oz (100g) ball
- Small amount of Tiger's Eye 4471 (brown and cream) (E)

Small amount of pink light worsted (DK) weight yarn (F)

Small amount of black light worsted (DK) weight yarn (G)

Black sewing thread (optional)

1 3/16in (30mm) safety nose

Small amount of toy fiberfill

Pair of 1in (24mm) safety eyes

Hairspray (optional)

16 x 16in (40 x 40cm) pillow form

HOOK AND EQUIPMENT
US J-10 (6mm) crochet hook
Stitch marker
Yarn needle
Pins
Stiff brush or pet brush

FINISHED SIZE
18 x 18in (45.5 x 45.5cm)

ABBREVIATIONS
See page 142.

PILLOW FRONT AND BACK
(make 2)
Row 1: Using A, ch40.
Row 2: 1dc in 3rd ch from hook (missed 2 ch do not count as dc), 1dc in each ch to end. (*38 sts*)
Rows 3–20: Ch3 (counts as first dc), 1dc in next dc, 1dc in each dc to end.
Fasten off.

HEAD
Round 1: Using B and a strand of black sewing thread held together (optional), ch4, join with a sl st to form a ring.
Round 2: Ch3 (counts as first dc), 11dc in ring, join with a sl st. (*12 sts*)
Round 3: Ch3, 1dc in same dc, [2 dc in next dc] to end, join with a sl st. (*24 sts*)
Round 4: Ch3, 2dc in next dc, [1dc in next dc, 2dc in next dc] to end, join with a sl st. (*36 sts*)
Round 5: Ch3, 1dc in next dc, 2dc in next dc, [1dc in each of next 2 dc, 2dc in next dc] to end, join with a sl st. (*48 sts*)
Round 6: Ch3, 1dc in each of next 2 dc, 2dc in next dc, [1dc in each of next 3 dc, 2dc in next dc] to end, join with a sl st. (*60 sts*)
Fasten off.

SNOUT
Round 1: Using B and a strand of black sewing thread held together (optional), ch4, join with a sl st to form a ring.
Round 2: Ch1 (counts as first sc), 7sc in ring, join with a sl st. (*8 sts*)
Round 3: Ch1, 2sc in next sc, [1sc in next sc, 2sc in next sc] to end, join with a sl st. (*12 sts*)
Round 4: Ch1, 1sc in next sc, 1sc in each sc to end, join with a sl st.
Round 5: Ch1, 1sc in next sc, 2sc in next sc, [1sc in each of next 2 sc, 2sc in next sc] to end, join with a sl st. (*16 sts*)
Round 6: Ch1, 2sc in next sc, [1sc in next sc, 2sc in next sc] to end, join with a sl st. (*24 sts*)

Rounds 7–10: Ch1, 1sc in next sc, 1sc in each sc to end, join with a sl st.
Fasten off.

EARS
(make 2)
Row 1: Using B and a strand of black sewing thread held together (optional), ch2.
Row 2: 1sc in 2nd ch from hook (missed ch does not count as sc). (*1 st*)
Row 3: Ch1 (counts as first sc), 1sc in same sc. (*2 sts*)
Row 4: Ch1, 1sc in same sc, 1sc in each sc to end. (*3 sts*)
Row 5: Ch1, 1sc in same sc, 1sc in each sc to end. (*4 sts*)
Row 6: Ch1, 1sc in same sc, 1sc in each sc to end. (*5 sts*)
Row 7: Ch1, 1sc in same sc, 1sc in each sc to end. (*6 sts*)
Row 8: Ch1, 1sc in same sc, 1sc in each sc to end. (*7 sts*)
Row 9: Ch1, 1sc in same sc, 1sc in each sc to end. (*8 sts*)
Fasten off, leaving a length of yarn.

TONGUE
Row 1: Using F, ch4.
Row 2: 1sc in 2nd ch from hook (missed ch does not count as sc), 1sc in each of next 2 sc. (*3 sts*)
Row 3: Ch1 (counts as first sc), 1sc in next sc, 2sc in last sc. (*4 sts*)
Row 4: Ch1, 1sc in each of next 2 sc, 2sc in last sc. (*5 sts*)
Row 5: Sc2tog, 1sc in next sc, sc2tog. (*3 sts*)
Fasten off.

TO MAKE UP
Place back and front pieces together with wrong sides facing. Using A, work a single crochet seam (see page 140) around the three sides of the pillow leaving the remaining side open. Insert the pillow form and then continue the single crochet seam around the fourth edge to close the gap. For an even edging, ensure you end with a total stitch count that is a multiple of 4.

Edging for pillow
Round 1: Join D to any corner with a sc, miss next sc, 5dc in next sc, miss next sc, [1sc in next sc, miss next sc, 5dc in next sc, miss next sc] around all four sides of the pillow, join with a sl st to top of first sc.
Fasten off D, join A.
Round 2: Ch1 (counts as first sc), 1sc in next st, 1sc in each st to end, join with a sl st.
Fasten off.

APPLIQUÉ HEAD
Using G, embroider stitches (see page 141) for the mouth on the snout, using the photograph as a guide. Add the safety nose and secure with the back. Stuff the snout firmly and sew it to the head. Add the safety eyes using the photo as a guide for position and secure with safety backs (see page 141). Clip off the surplus eye posts if required to enable the appliqué to lay flat. Sew the ears to the top of the head using the photo as a guide for position. Sew the tongue protruding from the mouth.

ADDING FUR
Adding the fur on the face can be done in two ways, either with a crochet hook (see page 141) or threading each strand through with a yarn needle and then tying the ends in a knot close to the fabric. The needle is better for getting in small areas, such as around the eyes.

Face
Cut B, C, and E into approx. 6in (15cm) lengths. Working with two strands held together in varying combinations, start by adding lines of fur fringing around the base of the snout. The fur is worked from the center outward in a circle, with rounds approx. 1in (2.5cm) apart. When you get to the eyes, trim around the bottom of the eyes. Brush for the fluffy effect and trim to the length required. For the area above the eyes, cut the strands slightly longer and work the lines of fur fringing closer together to produce the furry head. Brush and trim to length required. Add a little fur to bottom of each ear if required.

Snout
Starting at the center of the snout at the back, work two lines of fur fringing from the back of the snout to the front to fall either side of the top of the snout. Work a further row around the nose at the center of the snout. Brush and trim to length required.

It may be beneficial to spray the appliqué head with hairspray to keep the yarn in place (optional).

Pin the appliqué head to the center of the pillow and then sew in place. Sew in all ends (see page 139).

The adorable West Highland White Terrier has charmed owners for many years, so what better than to make a soft cuddly pillow to remind you of this cute dog? This little Westie is crocheted in super bulky yarn, which is brushed to give the fur its soft and fluffy look.

west highland terrier pillow

SKILL RATING ● ● ○

YARN AND MATERIALS
King Cole Big Value Super Chunky (100% acrylic), super bulky (super chunky) weight yarn, 90yd (81m) per 3½oz (100g) ball
   4 balls of White 1758 (A)

Small amount of pink light worsted (DK) weight yarn (B)

Small amount of black light worsted (DK) weight yarn (C)

1 3/16in (30mm) safety nose

Small amount of toy fiberfill

Pair of 1in (24mm) safety eyes

12in (30cm) diameter pillow form or fiberfill

Hairspray (optional)

HOOK AND EQUIPMENT
US J-10 (6mm) crochet hook

Yarn needle

Stiff brush or pet brush

Stitch marker

FINISHED SIZE
Approx. 15in (38cm) diameter

ABBREVIATIONS
See page 142.

PILLOW FRONT AND BACK
(make 2)
Round 1: Using A, ch4, join with a sl st to form a ring.
Round 2: Ch3 (counts as first dc), 11dc in ring, join with a sl st. (*12 sts*)
Round 3: Ch3, 1dc in same dc, [2dc in next dc] to end, join with a sl st. (*24 sts*)
Round 4: Ch3, 2dc in next dc, [1dc in next dc, 2dc in next dc] to end, join with a sl st. (*36 sts*)
Round 5: Ch3, 1dc in next dc, 2dc in next dc, [1dc in each of next 2 dc, 2dc in next dc] to end, join with a sl st. (*48 sts*)
Round 6: Ch3, 1dc in each of next 2 dc, 2dc in next dc, [1dc in each of next 3 dc, 2dc in next dc] to end, join with a sl st. (*60 sts*)
Round 7: Ch3, 1dc in each of next 3 dc, 2dc in next dc, [1dc in each of next 4 dc, 2dc in next dc] to end, join with a sl st. (*72 sts*)
Round 8: Ch3, 1dc in each of next 4 dc, 2dc in next dc, [1dc in each of next 5 dc, 2dc in next dc] to end, join with a sl st. (*84 sts*)
Round 9: Ch3, 1dc in each of next 5 dc, 2dc in next dc, [1dc in each of next 6 dc, 2dc in next dc] to end, join with a sl st. (*96 sts*)
Fasten off.

SNOUT
Round 1: Using A, ch4, join with a sl st to form a ring.
Round 2: Ch1 (counts as first sc), 7sc in ring, join with a sl st. (*8 sts*)
Round 3: Ch1, 1sc in same sc, [2sc in next sc] to end, join with a sl st. (*16 sts*)
Round 4: Ch1, 2sc in next sc, [1sc in next sc, 2sc in next sc] to end, join with a sl st. (*24 sts*)
Rounds 5 and 6: Ch1, 1sc in next sc, 1sc in each sc to end, join with a sl st.
Round 7: Ch1, 1sc in next sc, 2sc in next sc, [1sc in each of next 2 sc, 2sc in next sc] to end, join with a sl st. (*32 sts*)
Rounds 8 and 9: Ch1, 1sc in next sc, 1sc in each sc to end, join with a sl st.
Fasten off, leaving a length of yarn for sewing to pillow.

INNER EARS
(make 2)
Row 1: Using B, ch2.
Row 2: 1sc in 2nd ch from hook (missed ch does not count as sc). (1 st)
Row 3: Ch1 (counts as first sc), 1sc in same sc. (2 sts)
Row 4: Ch1, 1sc in same sc, 1sc in each sc to end. (3 sts)
Row 5: Ch1, 1sc in same sc, 1sc in each sc to end. (4 sts)
Row 6: Ch1, 1sc in same sc, 1sc in each sc to end. (5 sts)
Row 7: Ch1, 1sc in same sc, 1sc in each sc to end. (6 sts)
Row 8: Ch1, 1sc in same sc, 1sc in each sc to end. (7 sts)
Row 9: Ch1, 1sc in same sc, 1sc in each sc to end. (8 sts)
Fasten off.

west highland terrier pillow

OUTER EARS
(make 2)
Row 1: Using A, ch2.
Row 2: 1sc in 2nd ch from hook (missed ch does not count as sc). (*1 st*)
Row 3: Ch1 (counts as first sc), 1sc in same sc. (*2 sts*)
Row 4: Ch1, 1sc in same sc, 1sc in each sc to end. (*3 sts*)
Row 5: Ch1, 1sc in same sc, 1sc in each sc to end. (*4 sts*)
Row 6: Ch1, 1sc in same sc, 1sc in each sc to end. (*5 sts*)
Row 7: Ch1, 1sc in same sc, 1sc in each sc to end. (*6 sts*)
Row 8: Ch1, 1sc in same sc, 1sc in each sc to end. (*7 sts*)
Row 9: Ch1, 1sc in same sc, 1sc in each sc to end. (*8 sts*)
Place inner ear on top of outer ear, join with sc all around, working through both layers and working 2sc in same space at each corner.
Using A, work a further round of sc around each ear, working 2sc in same space at each corner.
Fasten off.

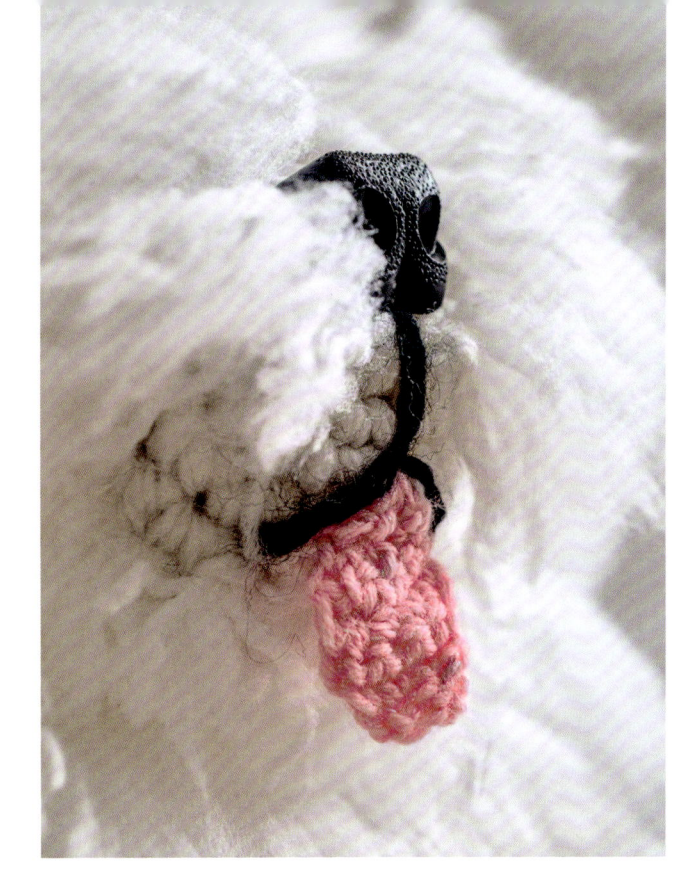

TONGUE
Row 1: Using B, ch4.
Row 2: 2sc in 2nd ch from hook (missed ch does not count as sc), 1sc in each sc to end. (*4 sts*)
Row 3: Ch1 (counts as first sc), 1sc in same sc, 1sc in each sc to end. (*5 sts*)
Rows 4 and 5: Ch1, 1sc in next sc, 1sc in each sc to end.
Fasten off.

TO MAKE UP
Place back and front pieces together with right sides facing. Using A, work a single crochet seam (see page 140) around leaving an opening of approx. 6in (15cm). Turn right side out.

Using C, sew the mouth markings onto snout (see page 141), using the photo as a guide. Insert the safety nose in position and secure with the back (see page 141). Stuff the snout and sew to the front of the pillow. Sew the tongue protruding from the mouth.

Add the safety eyes above the snout using the photo as a guide for position and secure with the backs. Sew the ears to the top of the head in the positions required.

Insert the pillow form and sew the gap closed.

ADDING FUR
Adding the fur on the face can be done in two ways, either with a crochet hook (see page 141) or threading each strand through with a yarn needle and then tying the ends in a knot close to the fabric. The needle is better for getting in small areas, such as around the eyes.

Face
Cut A into approx. 7in (18cm) lengths. Starting at the side of the snout, add a line of fur fringing all around the face. Add another round all around the face approx. 2in (5cm) away. Trim to length required. Brush the fringe all around for the fluffy effect.

Snout
Add lines of fur fringing on both sides of the snout from the center to the tip of the snout. Trim to the length required and brush for the fluffy effect.

It may be beneficial to spray pillow front with hairspray to keep the yarn in place (optional).

bearded collie pillow

The Bearded Collie is always a very popular family companion with its pretty face and big loving eyes. This pillow is crocheted in simple single and double crochet stitches and would make a perfect gift for any dog lover.

SKILL RATING ● ● ○

YARN AND MATERIALS
King Cole Big Value Super Chunky (100% acrylic), super bulky (super chunky) weight yarn, 90yd (81m) per 3½oz (100g) ball
- 2½ balls of Gray 24 (A)
- ½ ball of White 1758 (B)
- ½ ball of Graphite 1545 (dark gray) (C)
- Small amount of Latte 3490 (light brown) (D)

Small amount of black light worsted (DK) weight yarn (E)

1³⁄₁₆in (30mm) safety nose

Small amount of toy fiberfill

Pair of 1in (24mm) safety eyes

14in (35.5cm) diameter pillow form

Hairspray (optional)

HOOK AND EQUIPMENT
US J-10 (6mm) crochet hook
Yarn needle
Stiff brush or pet brush
Stitch marker

FINISHED SIZE
Approx. 15in (38cm) diameter

ABBREVIATIONS
See page 142.

bearded collie pillow 19

PILLOW FRONT AND BACK
(make 2)

Round 1: Using A, ch4, join with a sl st to form a ring.
Round 2: Ch3 (counts as first dc), 11dc in ring, join with a sl st. (*12 sts*)
Round 3: Ch3, 1dc in same dc, [2dc in next dc] to end, join with a sl st. (*24 sts*)
Round 4: Ch3, 2dc in next dc, [1dc in next dc, 2dc in next dc] to end, join with a sl st. (*36 sts*)
Round 5: Ch3, 1dc in next dc, 2dc in next dc, [1dc in each of next 2 dc, 2dc in next dc] to end, join with a sl st. (*48 sts*)
Round 6: Ch3, 1dc in each of next 2 dc, 2dc in next dc, [1dc in each of next 3 dc, 2dc in next dc] to end, join with a sl st. (*60 sts*)
Round 7: Ch3, 1dc in each of next 3 dc, 2dc in next dc, [1dc in each of next 4 dc, 2dc in next dc] to end, join with a sl st. (*72 sts*)
Round 8: Ch3, 1dc in each of next 4 dc, 2dc in next dc, [1dc in each of next 5 dc, 2dc in next dc] to end, join with a sl st. (*84 sts*)
Round 9: Ch3, 1dc in each of next 5 dc, 2dc in next dc, [1dc in each of next 6 dc, 2dc in next dc] to end, join with a sl st. (*96 sts*)
Fasten off.

SNOUT

Round 1: Using B, ch4, join with a sl st to form a ring.
Round 2: Ch1 (counts as first sc), 7sc in ring, join with a sl st. (*8 sts*)
Round 3: Ch1, 1sc in same sc, [2sc in next sc] to end, join with a sl st. (*16 sts*)
Round 4: Ch1, 1sc in next sc, 1sc in each sc to end, join with a sl st.
Round 5: Ch1, 2sc in next sc, [1sc in next sc, 2sc in next sc] to end, join with a sl st. (*24 sts*)
Round 6: Ch1, 1sc in next sc, 1sc in each sc to end, join with a sl st.
Round 7: Ch1, 1sc in each of next 2 sc, 2sc in next sc, [1sc in each of next 3 sc, 2sc in next sc] to end, join with a sl st. (*30 sts*)
Rounds 8-12: Ch1, 1sc in next sc, 1sc in each sc to end, join with a sl st.
Fasten off.

TO MAKE UP
Place back and front pieces together with right sides facing. Using A, work a single crochet seam (see page 140) around the pillow cover leaving an opening of approx. 6in (15cm). Turn right side out.

Using E, sew the mouth markings onto the snout (see page 141) using the photo as a guide. Insert the safety nose using the photo as a guide for position and secure with the back (see page 141). Stuff the snout lightly and sew to front of pillow in the position required.

Add the safety eyes above the snout in the positions required and secure with the backs.

Insert the pillow form, and then sew the opening closed.

ADDING FUR
Adding the fur on the face can be done in two ways, either with a crochet hook (see page 141) or threading each strand through with a yarn needle and then tying the ends into a knot close to the fabric. The needle is better for getting into small areas, such as around the eyes.

Ears
Cut lengths of C approx. 20in (50cm) long. Starting on one side of head, add a 2in (5cm) line of fur fringing to form the ear. Repeat on the other side. Gently unravel each length of yarn to give the fluffy effect and trim to length required.

Snout
Cut lengths of B approx. 10in (25cm) long. Start by adding a line of fur fringing along the top of the snout to the nose. Brush the fringe strands to give the fluffy effect and trim to the length required. Repeat on the other side. Continue to add fur fringing on either side. Trim any excess fur to produce the length required. Add a few lengths of D to the top of the snout and under chin. Brush and trim to the length required.

Lower face
Cut lengths of B approx. 5in (12.5cm) long, and work rows of fur to cover the bottom of the face and under the snout. Brush and trim in line with the bottom of the pillow. Trim to lengths required.

Rest of face
Cut lengths of A and B approx. 5in (12.5cm) long. Start at Row 6 of the snout and make a row of fringing along the bottom, then another row approx. 1in (2.5cm) below the first. Use some longer lengths around the edge of the face. Brush and trim. Continue around the rest of the face with A and B to design and color required. When working around the nose and eyes it may be easier to use a needle to add the yarn. Brush and trim to length required.

It may be beneficial to spray lightly with hairspray to keep the yarn in place (optional).

Being a Yorkshire Terrier owner myself, this pattern is an absolute must for any Yorkie lover. Crocheted throughout with worsted yarn in single and double crochet stitches, this adorable face is simple to create.

yorkshire terrier pillow

PILLOW FRONT AND BACK
(make 2)
Round 1: Using A, ch4, join with a sl st to form a ring.
Round 2: Ch3 (counts as first dc), 11dc in ring, join with a sl st. (*12 sts*)
Round 3: Ch3, 1dc in same dc, [2dc in next dc] to end, join with a sl st. (*24 sts*)
Round 4: Ch3, 2dc in next dc, [1dc in next dc, 2dc in next dc] to end, join with a sl st. (*36 sts*)
Round 5: Ch3, 1dc in next dc, 2dc in next dc, [1dc in each of next 2 dc, 2dc in next dc] to end, join with a sl st. (*48 sts*)
Round 6: Ch3, 1dc in each of next 2 dc, 2dc in next dc, [1dc in each of next 3 dc, 2dc in next dc] to end, join with a sl st. (*60 sts*)
Round 7: Ch3, 1dc in each of next 3 dc, 2dc in next dc, [1dc in each of next 4 dc, 2dc in next dc] to end, join with a sl st. (*72 sts*)
Round 8: Ch3, 1dc in each of next 4 dc, 2dc in next dc, [1dc in each of next 5 dc, 2dc in next dc] to end, join with a sl st. (*84 sts*)
Round 9: Ch3, 1dc in each of next 5 dc, 2dc in next dc, [1dc in each of next 6 dc, 2dc in next dc] to end, join with a sl st. (*96 sts*)
Round 10: Ch3, 1dc in each of next 6 dc, 2dc in next dc, [1dc in each of next 7 dc, 2dc in next dc] to end, join with a sl st. (*108 sts*)
Round 11: Ch3, 1dc in each of next 7 dc, 2dc in next dc, [1dc in each of next 8 dc, 2dc in next dc] to end, join with a sl st. (*120 sts*)
Round 12: Ch3, 1dc in each of next 8 dc, 2dc in next dc, [1dc in each of next 9 dc, 2dc in next dc] to end, join with a sl st. (*132 sts*)
Fasten off.

SNOUT
Round 1: Using A, ch4, join with a sl st to form a ring.
Round 2: Ch1 (counts as first sc), 7sc in ring, join with a sl st. (*8 sts*)
Round 3: Ch1, 2sc in next sc, [1sc in next sc, 2sc in next sc] to end, join with a sl st. (*12 sts*)
Round 4: Ch1, 1sc in next sc, 1sc in each sc to end, join with a sl st.
Round 5: Ch1, 1sc in next sc, 2sc in next sc, [1sc in each of next 2 sc, 2sc in next sc] to end, join with a sl st. (*16 sts*)
Round 6: Ch1, 2sc in next sc, [1sc in next sc, 2sc in next sc] to end, join with a sl st. (*24 sts*)
Round 7: Ch1, 1sc in each of next 2 sc, 2sc in next sc, [1sc in each of next 3 sc, 2sc in next sc] to end, join with a sl st. (*30 sts*)
Rounds 8–12: Ch1, 1sc in next sc, 1sc in each sc to end, join with a sl st.
Fasten off.

SKILL RATING ● ● ●

YARN AND MATERIALS
King Cole Bounty Aran (100% acrylic), worsted (Aran) weight yarn, 646yd (587m) per 8¾oz (250g) ball
  1 ball of Starling 1752 (A)

Small amount of pink bulky (chunky) weight yarn (B)

Small amount of black light worsted (DK) weight yarn (C)

1 3/16in (30mm) safety nose

Small amount of toy fiberfill

Pair of 1in (24mm) safety eyes

12in (30cm) diameter pillow form

Short length of ribbon

Hairspray (optional)

HOOK AND EQUIPMENT
US H-8 (5mm) crochet hook
Yarn needle
Stitch marker

FINISHED SIZE
Approx. 13in (33cm) diameter

ABBREVIATIONS
See page 142.

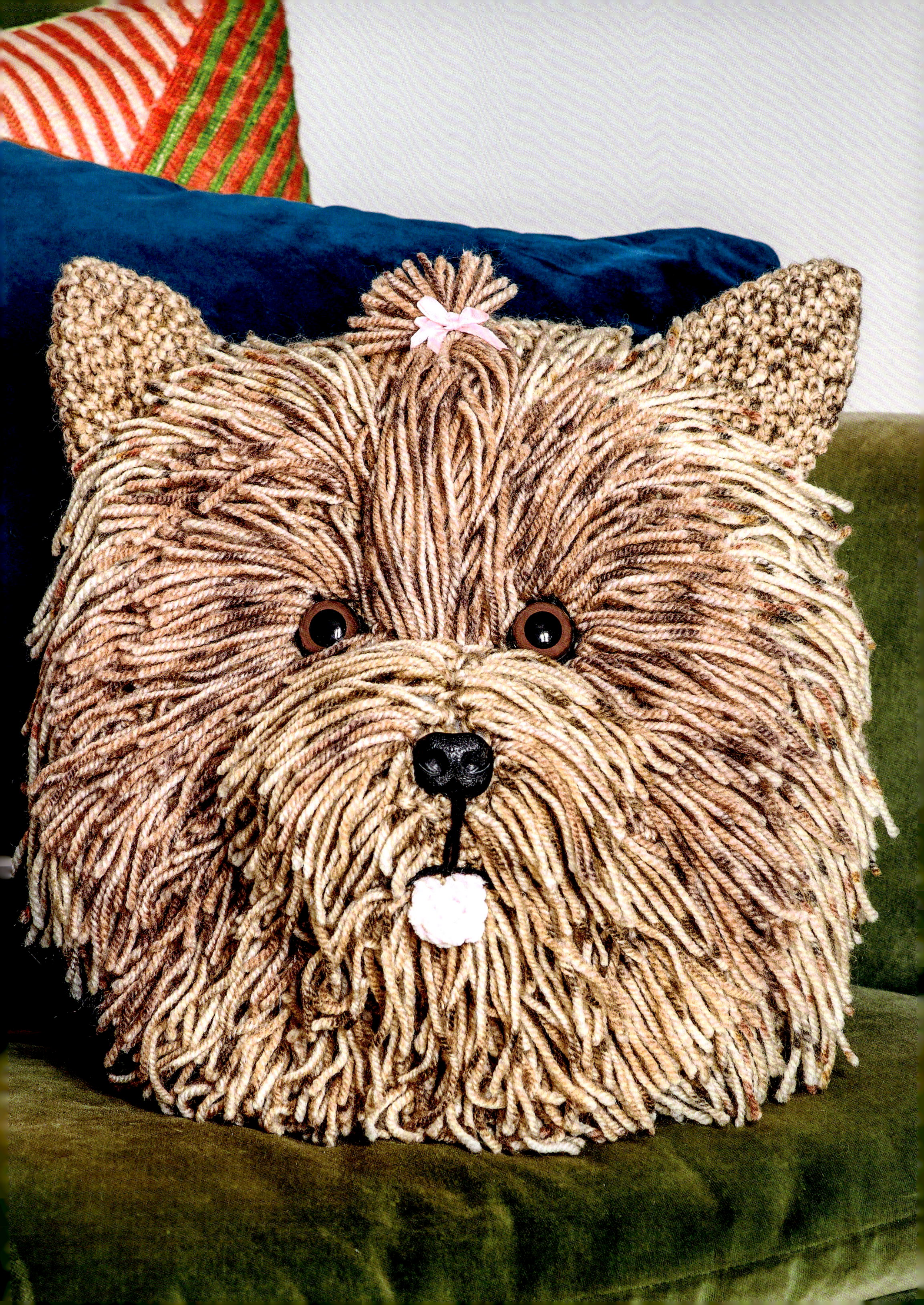

EARS
(make 2)
Round 1: Using A, ch4, join with a sl st to form a ring.
Round 2: Ch1 (counts as first sc), 7sc in ring, join with a sl st. (*8 sts*)
Round 3: Ch1, 2sc in next sc, [1sc in next sc, 2sc in next sc] to end, join with a sl st. (*12 sts*)
Round 4: Ch1, 1sc in next sc, 1sc in each sc to end, join with a sl st.
Round 5: Ch1, 1sc in next sc, 2sc in next sc, [1sc in each of next 2 sc, 2sc in next sc] to end, join with a sl st. (*16 sts*)
Round 6: Ch1, 1sc in next sc, 1sc in each sc to end, join with a sl st.
Round 7: Ch1, 1sc in each of next 2 sc, 2sc in next sc, [1sc in each of next 3 sc, 2sc in next sc] to end, join with a sl st. (*20 sts*)
Round 8: Ch1, 1sc in next sc, 1sc in each sc to end, join with a sl st.
Round 9: Ch1, 1sc in each of next 3 sc, 2sc in next sc, [1sc in each of next 4 sc, 2sc in next sc] to end, join with a sl st. (*24 sts*)
Rounds 10-12: Ch1, 1sc in next sc, 1sc in each sc to end, join with a sl st.
Fasten off.

TONGUE
Row 1: Using B, ch4.
Row 2: 1sc in 2nd ch from hook (missed ch does not count as sc), 1sc in each ch to end. (*3 sts*)
Rows 3 and 4: Ch1 (counts as first sc), 1sc in each of next 2 sc.
Fasten off.

TO MAKE UP
Place back and front pieces together with right sides facing. Using A, work a single crochet seam (see page 140) around the pillow cover leaving a gap of approx. 6in (15cm). Turn right side out.

Using C, embroider the mouth markings on the snout (see page 141). Add the safety nose and secure with the back (see page 141), then stuff the snout and sew to the front of the pillow. Sew the tongue protruding from the mouth. Sew the snout to the pillow using the photo as a guide.

Add the safety eyes above the snout using the photo as a guide and secure with the backs. Using C, sew a small border around each eye.

Fold each ear in half and sew the open seam together to form the ear. Sew ears to the top of the head in the positions required.

Insert the pillow form and sew the opening closed.

ADDING FUR
Adding the fur on the face can be done in two ways, either with a crochet hook (see page 141) or threading each strand through with a yarn needle and then tying the ends in a knot close to the fabric. The needle is better for getting in small areas, such as around the eyes.

Cut A into approx. 12in (30cm) lengths for the ponytail and 6in (15cm) lengths for the face. Start by adding several long strands of fur fringing above the snout for the ponytail. Tie with a ribbon and then use a length of A to sew the ponytail to the head. Using the shorter strands, continue to add lines of fur fringing around and under the snout, all around the face and around the ears. Trim to produce the length required.

It may be beneficial to spray pillow front with hairspray to keep the yarn in place (optional).

fluffy dog silhouette pillows

With their cheeky faces and bright backgrounds, this pair of fluffy dog pillows would add a gorgeous accent to any couch or bed. They are crocheted in super bulky yarn and finished with fur edging to complement the dogs' heads.

SKILL RATING ● ○ ○

YARN AND MATERIALS
King Cole Big Value Super Chunky (100% acrylic), super bulky (super chunky) weight yarn, 90yd (81m) per 3½oz (100g) ball
  2 balls of Red 9 or Pacific 1975 (blue) (A)

King Cole Tufty Super Chunky (100% polyester), super bulky (super chunky) weight yarn, 87yd (80m) per 7oz (200g) ball
  1 ball of White 2791 or Silver 2797 (gray) (B)

Small amount of black light worsted (DK) weight yarn (C)

1in (24mm) safety nose

Small amount of toy fiberfill

Pair of ⅞in (22mm) safety eyes

12in (30cm) diameter pillow form

HOOK AND EQUIPMENT
US J-10 (6mm) crochet hook

Stitch marker

Yarn needle

Pins

FINISHED SIZE
14in (35.5cm) diameter

ABBREVIATIONS
See page 142.

PATTERN NOTE
It is advisable to use a stitch marker with this pattern.

PILLOW FRONT AND BACK
(make 2)
Round 1: Using A, ch4, join with a sl st to form a ring.
Round 2: Ch3 (counts as first dc), 11dc in ring, join with a sl st. (*12 sts*)
Round 3: Ch3, 1dc in same dc, [2 dc in next dc] to end, join with a sl st. (*24 sts*)
Round 4: Ch3, 2dc in next dc, [1dc in next dc, 2dc in next dc] to end, join with a sl st. (*36 sts*)
Round 5: Ch3, 1dc in next dc, 2dc in next dc, [1dc in each of next 2 dc, 2dc in next dc] to end, join with a sl st. (*48 sts*)
Round 6: Ch3, 1dc in each of next 2 dc, 2dc in next dc, [1dc in each of next 3 dc, 2dc in next dc] to end, join with a sl st. (*60 sts*)
Round 7: Ch3, 1dc in each of next 3 dc, 2dc in next dc, [1dc in each of next 4 dc, 2dc in next dc] to end, join with a sl st. (*72 sts*)
Round 8: Ch3, 1dc in each of next 4 dc, 2dc in next dc, [1dc in each of next 5 dc, 2dc in next dc] to end, join with a sl st. (*84 sts*)
Round 9: Ch3, 1dcBLO in next dc, 1dcBLO in each dc to end, join with a sl st.
Fasten off.

DOG
FACE
Round 1: Using B, ch4, join with a sl st to form a ring.
Round 2: Ch1 (counts as first sc), 7sc in ring, join with a sl st. (*8 sts*)
Round 3: Ch1, 2sc in next sc, [1sc in next sc, 2sc in next sc] to end, join with a sl st. (*12 sts*)
Round 4: Ch1, 1sc in next sc, 2sc in next sc, [1sc in each of next 2 sc, 2sc in next sc] to end, join with a sl st. (*16 sts*)

Round 5: Ch1, 1sc in each of next 2 sc, 2sc in next sc, [1sc in each of next 3 sc, 2sc in next sc] to end, join with a sl st. (*20 sts*)
Round 6: Ch1, 1sc in each of next 3 sc, 2sc in next sc, [1sc in each of next 4 sc, 2sc in next sc] to end, join with a sl st. (*24 sts*)
Round 7: Ch1, 1sc in each of next 4 sc, 2sc in next sc, [1sc in each of next 5 sc, 2sc in next sc] to end, join with a sl st. (*28 sts*)
Fasten off.

SNOUT
Round 1: Using B, ch4, join with a sl st to form a ring.
Round 2: Ch1 (counts as first sc), 7sc in ring, join with a sl st. (*8 sts*)
Round 3: Ch1, 2sc in next sc, [1sc in next sc, 2sc in next sc] to end, join with a sl st. (*12 sts*)
Rounds 4 and 5: Ch1, 1sc in next sc, 1sc in each sc to end, join with a sl st.
Fasten off.

EARS
(make 2)
Row 1: Using B, ch6.
Row 2: 1sc in 2nd ch from hook (missed ch does not count as sc), 1sc in each ch to end. (*5 sts*)
Rows 3–7: Ch1 (counts as first sc), 1sc in next sc, 1sc in each sc to end. (*5 sts*)
Fasten off.

TO MAKE UP
Place back and front pieces together with right sides facing. Using A, work a single crochet seam around (see page 140), leaving an opening of approx. 6in (15cm). Turn right side out. Insert the pillow form, and then sew the opening closed. Using B, work one round of single crochet around the outer edge to give the fluffy edging to the pillow.

Dog face
Using C, sew the mouth markings onto the snout using the photo as a guide (see page 141).

Insert the safety nose in the position required and secure with the back (see page 141). Stuff and sew the snout to the front of the face. Add safety eyes above the snout and secure with the backs.

Sew the head to the center of the pillow. Pin ears to the pillow on either side of the head and then sew in place.

fluffy dog silhouette pillows **27**

Spaniels are happy and energetic dogs who love to cuddle, and this cute pillow is the next best thing. Made using double and single crochet stitches and with fur on the front and back, this pillow would take pride of place on any chair or couch and is perfect to cuddle up to on a cold winter's night.

brown spaniel pillow

SKILL RATING ● ● ○

YARN AND MATERIALS
King Cole Big Value Super Chunky (100% acrylic), super bulky (super chunky) weight yarn, 90yd (81m) per 3½oz (100g) ball
- 5 balls of Brown 31 (A)
- ½ ball of Champagne 12 (white) (B)

Small amount of black bulky (chunky) weight yarn (C)

1 3/16in (30mm) safety nose
Small amount of toy fiberfill
Pair of 1in (24mm) safety eyes
16 x 16in (40 x 40cm) pillow form

HOOK AND EQUIPMENT
US J-10 (6mm) crochet hook
Yarn needle
Stitch marker

FINISHED SIZE
18 x 18in (45.5 x 45.5cm)

ABBREVIATIONS
See page 142.

PILLOW FRONT AND BACK
(make 2)
Row 1: Using A, ch36.
Row 2: 1dc in 3rd ch from hook (missed 2 ch does not count as dc), 1dc in each ch to end. (*34 sts*)
Rows 3–17: Ch3 (counts as first dc), 1dc in next dc, 1dc in each dc to end.
Fasten off.

SNOUT
Round 1: Using B, ch4, join with a sl st to form a ring.
Round 2: Ch1 (counts as first sc), 7sc in ring, join with a sl st. (*8 sts*)
Round 3: Ch1, 1sc in same sc, [2sc in next sc] to end, join with a sl st. (*16 sts*)
Round 4: Ch1, 1sc in next sc, 1sc in each sc to end, join with a sl st.
Round 5: Ch1, 2sc in next sc, [1sc in next sc, 2sc in next sc] to end, join with a sl st. (*24 sts*)
Round 6: Ch1, 1sc in next sc, 1sc in each sc to end, join with a sl st.
Round 7: Ch1, 1sc in next sc, 2sc in next sc, [1sc in each of next 2 sc, 2sc in next sc] to end, join with a sl st. (*30 sts*)
Round 8: Ch1, 1sc in next sc, 1sc in each sc to end, join with a sl st.
Fasten off.

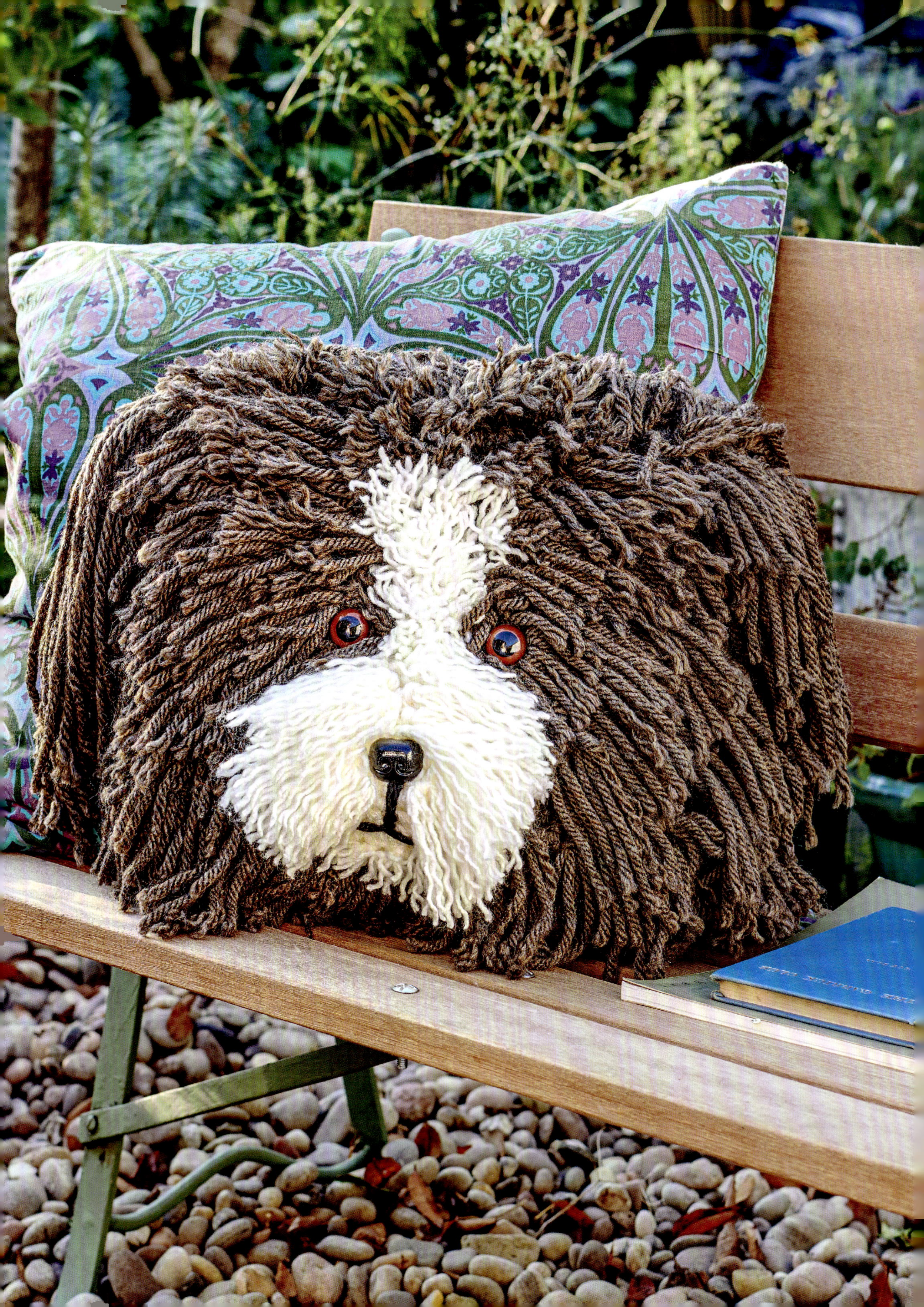

TO MAKE UP
Place back and front pieces together with right sides facing. Using A, work a single crochet seam (see page 140) around the pillow cover leaving a gap of approx. 6in (15cm). Turn right side out.

Using C, embroider the mouth markings onto the snout (see page 141) using the photo as a guide. Add the safety nose to the snout and secure with the back (see page 141). Stuff the snout and sew to the front of the pillow using the photo as a guide for position. Add the safety eyes and secure with the backs. Clip off the surplus eye posts.

Insert the pillow form and use a single crochet seam to close the gap.

ADDING FUR
Adding the fur on the face can be done in two ways, either with a crochet hook (see page 141) or threading each strand through with a yarn needle and then tying the ends into a knot close to the fabric. The needle is better for getting into small areas, such as around the eyes.

Pillow back
Cut A into approx. 7in (18cm) lengths. Starting approx. 3in (7.5cm) from the bottom of the pillow, add lines of fur fringing approx. 2in (5cm) apart until you reach the top of the pillow.

Snout
Cut B into approx. 7in (18cm) lengths. Add lines of fur fringing of yarn on both sides of the snout from the center to the tip of the snout. Separate the plies to create extra fluffy fur. Trim and shape to your preference.

Rest of pillow front
Cut B into approx. 3in (7.5cm) lengths. Add a fur section above the snout all the way to the top of the pillow, approx. 1in (2.5cm) wide. Separate the plies to create extra fluffy fur. Trim to your preference.

Cut A into approx. 7in (18cm) lengths and continue to fill in the front of the pillow and around the eyes. Trim to shape, level with the bottom of the pillow on both sides. Trim around the eyes as required.

husky pillow

With its piercing blue eyes, this lovely round Husky pillow gives you the feeling you are actually sitting with your dog. The yarn is brushed to give super-soft fur on both sides of the pillow, which you can snuggle up to on the couch. Both sides of the pillow are crocheted in double crochet stitches, with the snout and ears worked in single crochet stitches.

SKILL RATING ● ● ○

YARN AND MATERIALS
King Cole Big Value Super Chunky (100% acrylic), super bulky (super chunky) weight yarn, 90yd (81m) per 3½oz (100g) ball
  3 balls of Gray 24 (A)
  1 ball of White 1758 (B)

Small amount of black light worsted (DK) weight yarn (C)
1³⁄₁₆in (30mm) safety nose
Small amount of toy fiberfill
Pair of 1in (24mm) safety eyes in blue
14in (35.5cm) diameter pillow form
Hairspray (optional)

HOOK AND EQUIPMENT
US J-10 (6mm) crochet hook
Stitch marker
Yarn needle
Stiff brush or pet brush

FINISHED SIZE
Approx. 15in (38cm) diameter

ABBREVIATIONS
See page 142.

husky pillow **31**

PILLOW FRONT AND BACK
(make 2)
Round 1: Using A, ch4, join with a sl st to form a ring.
Round 2: Ch3 (counts as first dc), 11dc in ring, join with a sl st in first dc. (*12 sts*)
Round 3: Ch3, 1dc in same dc, [2dc in next dc] to end, join with a sl st. (*24 sts*)
Round 4: Ch3, 2dc in next dc, [1dc in next dc, 2dc in next dc] to end, join with a sl st. (*36 sts*)
Round 5: Ch3, 1dc in next dc, 2dc in next dc, [1dc in each of next 2 dc, 2dc in next dc] to end, join with a sl st. (*48 sts*)
Round 6: Ch3, 1dc in each of next 2 dc, 2dc in next dc, [1dc in each of next 3 dc, 2dc in next dc] to end, join with a sl st. (*60 sts*)
Round 7: Ch3, 1dc in each of next 3 dc, 2dc in next dc, [1dc in each of next 4 dc, 2dc in next dc] to end, join with a sl st. (*72 sts*)
Round 8: Ch3, 1dc in each of next 4 dc, 2dc in next dc, [1dc in each of next 5 dc, 2dc in next dc] to end, join with a sl st. (*84 sts*)
Round 9: Ch3, 1dcBLO in next dc, 1dcBLO in each dc to end, join with a sl st.
Round 10: Ch3, 1dc in each of next 10 dc, 2dc in next dc, [1dc in each of next 7 dc, 2dc in next dc] to end, join with a sl st. (*94 sts*)
Fasten off.

SNOUT
Round 1: Using B, ch4, join with a sl st to form a ring.
Round 2: Ch1 (counts as first sc), 7sc in ring, join with a sl st. (*8 sts*)
Round 3: Ch1, 1sc in next sc, 1sc in each sc to end, join with a sl st.
Round 4: Ch1, 2sc in next sc, [1sc in next sc, 2sc in next sc] to end, join with a sl st. (*12 sts*)
Round 5: Ch1, 1sc in next sc, 1sc in each sc to end, join with a sl st.
Round 6: Ch1, 2sc in next sc, [1sc in next sc, 2sc in next sc] to end, join with a sl st. (*18 sts*)
Round 7: Ch1, 1sc in next sc, 1sc in each sc to end, join with a sl st.
Round 8: Ch1, 1sc in next sc, 2sc in next sc, [1sc in each of next 2 sc, 2sc in next sc] to end, join with a sl st. (*24 sts*)
Round 9: Ch1, 1sc in next sc, 1sc in each sc to end, join with a sl st.
Round 10: Ch1, 1sc in each of next 2 sc, 2sc in next sc, [1sc in each of next 3 sc, 2sc in next sc] to end, join with a sl st. (*30 sts*)
Rounds 11-14: Ch1, 1sc in next sc, 1sc in each sc to end, join with a sl st.
Fasten off.

INNER EARS
(make 2)
Row 1: Using B, ch2.
Row 2: 2sc in 2nd ch from hook (missed ch does not count as sc). (*2 sts*)
Row 3: Ch1 (counts as first sc), 1sc in same sc, 1sc in each sc to end. (*3 sts*)
Row 4: Ch1, 1sc in same sc, 1sc in each sc to end. (*4 sts*)
Row 5: Ch1, 1sc in same sc, 1sc in each sc to end. (*5 sts*)
Row 6: Ch1, 1sc in same sc, 1sc in each sc to end. (*6 sts*)
Row 7: Ch1, 1sc in same sc, 1sc in each sc to end. (*7 sts*)
Row 8: Ch1, 1sc in same sc, 1sc in each sc to end. (*8 sts*)
Row 9: Ch1, 1sc in same sc, 1sc in each sc to end. (*9 sts*)
Fasten off.

OUTER EAR
(make 2)
Row 1: Using A, ch2.
Row 2: 2sc in 2nd ch from hook (missed ch does not count as sc). (*2 sts*)
Rows 3-9: Work as inner ear. (*9 sts*)
Row 10: Place inner ear on top of outer ear and work a single crochet seam all around to join ears, working 2sc in tip of ear, join with a sl st.
Fasten off.
With inner ear facing, join A at bottom right corner of ear.
Rows 11-13: Ch1, 1sc in next sc, 1 sc in each sc to tip of ear, 2 sc in next sc, 1 sc in each sc to bottom left corner of ear, turn.
Fasten off.

TO MAKE UP
Place the front and back with right sides together. Using A, work a single crochet seam around (see page 140), leaving an opening of approx. 6in (15cm). Turn right side out.

Using C, sew the mouth markings onto the snout (see page 141) using the photo as a guide. Insert the safety nose and secure with the back (see page 141). Stuff the snout firmly and sew to the front of the pillow in the position required.

Add the eyes above the snout and secure with the backs. Sew the ears to the pillow using the photo as a guide.

Insert the pillow form, and then sew the opening closed.

ADDING FUR
Adding the fur on the face can be done in two ways, either with a crochet hook (see page 141) or threading each strand through with a yarn needle and then tying the ends into a knot close to the fabric. The fur is added to both sides of the pillow, working the back of the pillow first, then moving on to the front. The needle is better for getting into small areas, such as around the eyes.

Back
Cut lengths of A and B approx. 7in (18cm) long. Starting approx. 3in (7.5cm) from the bottom of the pillow, work a line of fur fringing across the back in A. Continue working rows approx. 2in (5cm) apart, until you reach the top of the pillow. Brush with a stiff brush or pet brush to give the fluffy look. Trim to shape, in line with the bottom of the pillow.

Front
Starting around the snout, work a round of fur fringing in B. Work a further two rounds of fur fringing approx. 1in (2.5cm) apart. Brush and trim around the eyes as required. Change to A and continue to work in rounds of fur fringe until the whole front of the pillow is covered. Brush and trim to shape.

It may be beneficial to spray with hairspray to keep the fur in place (optional).

The highly popular and faithful Border Collie is always a family favorite. This pillow is crocheted in black and white super bulky yarn in single and double crochet stitches. You can easily customize it to resemble your own pet by changing the yarn shades.

border collie pillow

SKILL RATING ● ● ○

YARN AND MATERIALS
King Cole Big Value Super Chunky (100% acrylic), super bulky (super chunky) weight yarn, 90yd (81m) per 3½oz (100g) ball
    3 balls of Black 8 (A)
    1 ball of White 1758 (B)

1³⁄₁₆in (30mm) safety nose
Small amount of toy fiberfill
Pair of 1in (24mm) safety eyes
12in (30cm) diameter pillow form
Hairspray (optional)

HOOK AND EQUIPMENT
US J-10 (6mm) crochet hook
Stitch marker
Yarn needle
Stiff brush or pet brush

FINISHED SIZE
Approx. 13in (33cm) in diameter

ABBREVIATIONS
See page 142.

PILLOW FRONT AND BACK
(make 2)
Round 1: Using A, ch4, join with a sl st to form a ring.
Round 2: Ch3 (counts as first dc), 11dc in ring, join with a sl st. (*12 sts*)
Round 3: Ch3, 1dc in same dc, [2dc in next dc] to end, join with a sl st. (*24 sts*)
Round 4: Ch3, 2dc in next dc, [1dc in next dc, 2dc in next dc] to end, join with a sl st. (*36 sts*)
Round 5: Ch3, 1dc in next dc, 2dc in next dc, [1dc in each of next 2 dc, 2dc in next dc] to end, join with a sl st. (*48 sts*)
Round 6: Ch3, 1dc in each of next 2 dc, 2dc in next dc, [1dc in each of next 3 dc, 2dc in next dc] to end, join with a sl st. (*60 sts*)
Round 7: Ch3, 1dc in each of next 3 dc, 2dc in next dc, [1dc in each of next 4 dc, 2dc in next dc] to end, join with a sl st. (*72 sts*)
Round 8: Ch3, 1dc in each of next 4 dc, 2dc in next dc, [1dc in each of next 5 dc, 2dc in next dc] to end, join with a sl st. (*84 sts*)
Round 9: Ch3, 1dcBLO in next dc, 1dcBLO in each dc to end, join with a sl st.
Fasten off.

SNOUT
Round 1: Using B, ch4, join with a sl st to form a ring.
Round 2: Ch1 (counts as first sc), 7sc in ring, join with a sl st. (*8 sts*)
Round 3: Ch1, 2sc in next sc, [1sc in next sc, 2sc in next sc] to end, join with a sl st. (*12 sts*)
Round 4: Ch1, 1sc in next sc, 2sc in next sc, [1sc in each of next 2 sc, 2sc in next sc] to end, join with a sl st. (*16 sts*)
Rounds 5 and 6: Ch1, 1sc in next sc, 1sc in each sc to end, join with a sl st.
Round 7: Ch1, 1sc in each of next 2 sc, 2sc in next sc, [1sc in each of next 3 sc, 2sc in next sc] to end, join with a sl st. (*20 sts*)
Round 8: Ch1, 1sc in next sc, 1sc in each sc to end, join with a sl st.
Round 9: Ch1, 1sc in each of next 3 sc, 2sc in next sc, [1sc in each of next 4 sc, 2sc in next sc] to end, join with a sl st. (*24 sts*)
Rounds 10-12: Ch1, 1sc in next sc, 1sc in each sc to end, join with a sl st.
Fasten off.

EARS
(make 4)
Row 1: Using A, ch2.
Row 2: 1sc in 2nd ch from hook (missed ch does not count as sc). (*1 st*)
Row 3: Ch1 (counts as first sc), 1sc in same sc. (*2 sts*)
Row 4: Ch1, 1sc in same sc, 1sc in each sc to end. (*3 sts*)
Row 5: Ch1, 1sc in same sc, 1sc in each sc to end. (*4 sts*)
Row 6: Ch1, 1sc in same sc, 1sc in each sc to end. (*5 sts*)
Row 7: Ch1, 1sc in same sc, 1sc in each sc to end. (*6 sts*)
Row 8: Ch1, 1sc in same sc, 1sc in each sc to end. (*7 sts*)
Row 9: Ch1, 1sc in same sc, 1sc in each sc to end. (*8 sts*)
Row 10: Ch1, 1sc in same sc, 1sc in each sc to end. (*9 sts*)
Rows 11-14: Ch1, 1sc in next sc, 1sc in each sc to end.
Row 15: Sc2tog, 1sc in each sc to last 2 sc, sc2tog. (*7 sts*)
Fasten off.

TO MAKE UP

Place back and front pieces together with right sides facing. Using A, work a single crochet seam around (see page 140), leaving an opening of approx. 6in (15cm). Turn right side out.

Using A, sew the mouth markings onto the snout (see page 141) using the photo as a guide. Insert the safety nose and secure with the back (see page 141). Stuff the snout lightly and sew to the front of the pillow in the position required.

Add the safety eyes in the positions required and secure with the backs.

Place two ear pieces together and crochet one round of single crochet evenly around the whole edge to join the two pieces, leaving a length of yarn for sewing to the head. Repeat with the other two pieces. Sew the ears to the head on each side, using the photo as a guide.

Insert the pillow form, and then sew the opening closed.

ADDING FUR

Adding the fur on the face can be done in two ways, either with a crochet hook (see page 141) or threading each strand through with a yarn needle and then tying the ends into a knot close to the fabric. The needle is better for getting into small areas, such as around the eyes.

Cut lengths of B approx. 7in (18cm) long. Starting under the snout, add a line of fur fringing under the snout. Work another couple of lines above the snout approx. 2in (5cm) apart.

Cut lengths of A approx. 7in (18cm) long, and add lines of fringing on each side of the snout, then add a further line of fringing approx. 2in (5cm) away on each side of the face.

Brush the fringe all around for the fluffy effect and trim to the length required.

It may be beneficial to spray with hairspray to hold the yarn in place (optional).

bichon frisé pillow

This adorable fluffy little dog is always happy and playful as depicted in this pretty pillow, which will take pride of place in any living room. The two sides of the pillow are crocheted in double crochet stitches separately and then joined together with super bulky yarn, making it easy to brush to give the fluffy look. The snout is worked in single crochet stitches.

SKILL RATING ● ● ○

YARN AND MATERIALS
King Cole Big Value Super Chunky (100% acrylic), super bulky (super chunky) weight yarn, 90yd (81m) per 3½oz (100g) ball
4 balls of Champagne 12 (white) (A)

Small amount of black light worsted (DK) weight yarn (B)

1 3/16in (30mm) safety nose

Toy fiberfill

Pair of 1in (24mm) safety eyes

12in (30cm) diameter pillow form

Hairspray (optional)

HOOK AND EQUIPMENT
US size K-10½ (6.5mm) crochet hook

Stitch marker

Yarn needle

Stiff brush or pet brush

FINISHED SIZE
Approx 14in (35.5cm) diameter

ABBREVIATIONS
See page 142.

PILLOW FRONT AND BACK
(make 2)
Round 1: Using A, ch4, join with a sl st to form a ring.
Round 2: Ch3 (counts as first dc), 11dc in ring, join with a sl st. (*12 sts*)
Round 3: Ch3, 1dc in same dc, [2dc in next dc] to end, join with a sl st. (*24 sts*)
Round 4: Ch3, 2dc in next dc, [1dc in next dc, 2dc in next dc] to end, join with a sl st. (*36 sts*)
Round 5: Ch3, 1dc in next dc, 2dc in next dc, [1dc in each of next 2 dc, 2dc in next dc] to end, join with a sl st. (*48 sts*)
Round 6: Ch3, 1dc in each of next 2 dc, 2dc in next dc, [1dc in each of next 3 dc, 2dc in next dc] to end, join with a sl st. (*60 sts*)

Round 7: Ch3, 1dc in each of next 3 dc, 2dc in next dc, [1dc in each of next 4 dc, 2dc in next dc] to end, join with a sl st. (72 sts)
Round 8: Ch3, 1dc in each of next 4 dc, 2dc in next dc, [1dc in each of next 5 dc, 2dc in next dc] to end, join with a sl st. (84 sts)
Round 9: Ch3, 1dc in each of next 5 dc, 2dc in next dc, [1dc in each of next 6 dc, 2dc in next dc] to end, join with a sl st. (96 sts)
Fasten off.

BICHON FRISÉ
SNOUT
Round 1: Using A, ch4, join with a sl st to form a ring.
Round 2: Ch1 (counts as first sc), 7sc in ring, join with a sl st. (8 sts)
Round 3: Ch1, 2sc in next sc, [1sc in next sc, 2sc in next sc] to end, join with a sl st. (12 sts)
Round 4: Ch1, 1sc in next sc, 2sc in next sc, [1sc in each of next 2 sc, 2sc in next sc] to end, join with a sl st. (16 sts)
Round 5: Ch1, 1sc in next sc, 1sc in each sc to end, join with a sl st.
Round 6: Ch1, 2sc in next sc, [1sc in next sc, 2sc in next sc] to end, join with a sl st. (24 sts)
Rounds 7–12: Ch1, 1sc in next sc, 1sc in each sc to end, join with a sl st.
Fasten off.

TO MAKE UP
Place the front and back with right sides together and work a single crochet seam around (see page 140), leaving an opening of approx. 6in (15cm). Turn right side out.

Using B, sew the nose markings onto the snout (see page 141), using the photo as a guide. Insert the safety nose and secure with the back. Stuff the snout firmly and sew to the front of the pillow in the position required.

Add the eyes above the snout and secure with the backs through the gap in the pillow (see page 141). Insert the pillow form, and then sew the opening closed. Sew in any loose ends (see page 139).

ADDING FUR
Adding the fur on the face can be done in two ways, either with a crochet hook (see page 141) or threading each strand through with a yarn needle and then tying the ends into a knot close to the fabric. The needle is better for getting into small areas, such as around the eyes.

Snout
Cut lengths of A approx. 6in (15cm) long. Start by adding a line of fur fringing along the top of the snout to the nose (see page 141). Brush the fringe strands with a stiff brush or pet brush to give the fluffy effect and trim to the length required. Repeat on the other side. Continue to add fur fringing on either side. Trim any excess fur to produce the length required. Continue in this manner all around the snout.

Ears
Cut lengths of A approx. 10in (25cm) long. Starting at one of the top corners of the front of the pillow attach five or six fur fringes to form the ears. The more yarn used, the more the ears will stand out. Work the other ear in the opposite corner. Brush both ears to give the fluffy look. Trim to the length required.

Rest of face
Cut lengths of A approx. 6in (15cm) long and continue to add lines of fur fringing all around the front of the pillow. For the fluffy area above the forehead add the fringe as close together as you can, starting in lines above the snout. Add more yarn to this area and leave it a little longer than the rest of the face. Brush forward each time to give the fluffy effect. Continue upward from the forehead with more lines kept close together to create as much fur as possible. Trim across the front of the forehead to the length required and then brush.

It may be beneficial to spray lightly with hairspray to keep the yarn in place (optional).

The loyal and obedient German Shepherd is a firm favorite among dog lovers. This pillow, with its friendly face and faithful eyes, will make a great addition to any chair or couch. It's worked in super bulky yarn using single and double crochet stitches, and the varied colors in the face enable you to make the pillow resemble your own dog.

german shepherd pillow

SKILL RATING ● ● ○

YARN AND MATERIALS
King Cole Big Value Super Chunky (100% acrylic), super bulky (super chunky) weight yarn, 90yd (81m) per 3½oz (100g) ball
- 3 balls of Latte 3490 (light brown) (A)
- 1 ball of Black 8 (B)
- ½ ball of Brass 3400 (light brown) (C)

Small amount of pink bulky (chunky) weight yarn (D)

Small amount of gray bulky (chunky) weight yarn (E)

1 3/16in (30mm) safety nose

Small amount of toy fiberfill

Pair of 1in (24mm) safety eyes

14in (35.5cm) pillow form

Hairspray (optional)

HOOK AND EQUIPMENT
US J-10 (6mm) crochet hook
Stitch marker
Yarn needle
Stiff brush or pet brush

FINISHED SIZE
17 x 15in (43 x 38cm)

ABBREVIATIONS
See page 142.

PILLOW FRONT AND BACK
(make 2)
Round 1: Using A, ch4, join with a sl st to form a ring.
Round 2: Ch3 (counts as first dc), 11dc in ring, join with a sl st. (*12 sts*)
Round 3: Ch3, 1dc in same dc, [2dc in next dc] to end, join with a sl st. (*24 sts*)
Round 4: Ch3, 2dc in next dc, [1dc in next dc, 2dc in next dc] to end, join with a sl st. (*36 sts*)
Round 5: Ch3, 1dc in next dc, 2dc in next dc, [1dc in each of next 2 dc, 2dc in next dc] to end, join with a sl st. (*48 sts*)
Round 6: Ch3, 1dc in each of next 2 dc, 2dc in next dc, [1dc in each of next 3 dc, 2dc in next dc] to end, join with a sl st. (*60 sts*)
Round 7: Ch3, 1dc in each of next 3 dc, 2dc in next dc, [1dc in each of next 4 dc, 2dc in next dc] to end, join with a sl st. (*72 sts*)
Round 8: Ch3, 1dc in each of next 4 dc, 2dc in next dc, [1dc in each of next 5 dc, 2dc in next dc] to end, join with a sl st. (*84 sts*)
Round 9: Ch3, 1dc in each of next 5 dc, 2dc in next dc, [1dc in each of next 6 dc, 2dc in next dc] to end, join with a sl st. (*96 sts*)
Fasten off.

SNOUT INNER
Round 1: Using B, ch4, join with a sl st to form a ring.
Round 2: Ch1 (counts as first sc), 7sc in ring, join with a sl st. (*8 sts*)
Round 3: Ch1, 2sc in next sc, [1sc in next sc, 2sc in next sc] to end, join with a sl st. (*12 sts*)
Round 4: Ch1, 1sc in next sc, 2sc in next sc, [1sc in each of next 2 sc, 2sc in next sc] to end, join with a sl st. (*16 sts*)
Round 5: Ch1, 1sc in each of next 2 sc, 2sc in next sc, [1sc in each of next 3 sc, 2sc in next sc] to end, join with a sl st. (*20 sts*)
Round 6: Ch1, 1sc in each of next 3 sc, 2sc in next sc, [1sc in each of next 4 sc, 2sc in next sc] to end, join with a sl st. (*24 sts*)
Rounds 7–12: Ch1, 1sc in next sc, 1sc in each sc to end, join with a sl st.
Fasten off.

JOWLS
Row 1: Using B, ch6.
Row 2: 1sc in 2nd ch from hook (missed ch does not count as sc), 1sc in each ch to end. (5 sts)
Row 3: Ch1 (counts as first sc), 1sc in same sc, 1sc in each sc to end. (6 sts)
Row 4: Ch1, 1sc in same sc, 1sc in each sc to end. (7 sts)
Row 5: Ch1, 1sc in same sc, 1sc in each sc to end. (8 sts)
Row 6: Ch1, 1sc in same sc, 1sc in each sc to end. (9 sts)
Row 7: Ch1, 1sc in same sc, 1sc in each sc to end. (10 sts)
Row 8: Ch1, 1sc in same sc, 1sc in each sc to end. (11 sts)
Row 9: Ch1, 1sc in same sc, 1sc in each sc to end. (12 sts)
Rows 10–23: Ch1, 1sc in next sc, 1sc in each sc to end.
Row 24: Ch1, 1sc in next sc, 1sc in each sc to last 2 sts, sc2tog. (11 sts)
Row 25: Ch1, 1sc in next sc, 1sc in each sc to last 2 sts, sc2tog. (10 sts)
Row 26: Ch1, 1sc in next sc, 1sc in each sc to last 2 sts, sc2tog. (9 sts)

german shepherd pillow

Row 27: Ch1, 1sc in next sc, 1sc in each sc to last 2 sts, sc2tog. (*8 sts*)
Row 28: Ch1, 1sc in next sc, 1sc in each sc to last 2 sts, sc2tog. (*7 sts*)
Row 29: Ch1, 1sc in next sc, 1sc in each sc to last 2 sts, sc2tog. (*6 sts*)
Row 30: Ch1, 1sc in next sc, 1sc in each sc to end.
Fasten off.

EARS
(make 4)
Row 1: Using A, ch2.
Row 2: 1sc in 2nd ch from hook (missed ch does not count as sc). (*1 st*)
Row 3: Ch1 (counts as first sc), 1sc in same sc. (*2 sts*)
Row 4: Ch1, 1sc in same sc, 1sc in each sc to end. (*3 sts*)
Row 5: Ch1, 1sc in same sc, 1sc in each sc to end. (*4 sts*)
Row 6: Ch1, 1sc in next sc, 1sc in each sc to end.
Row 7: Ch1, 1sc in same sc, 1sc in each sc to end. (*5 sts*)
Row 8: Ch1, 1sc in next sc, 1sc in each sc to end.
Row 9: Ch1, 1sc in same sc, 1sc in each sc to end. (*6 sts*)
Row 10: Ch1, 1sc in next sc, 1sc in each sc to end.
Row 11: Ch1, 1sc in same sc, 1sc in each sc to end. (*7 sts*)
Row 12: Ch1, 1sc in next sc, 1sc in each sc to end.
Row 13: Ch1, 1sc in same sc, 1sc in each sc to end. (*8 sts*)
Row 14: Ch1, 1sc in next sc, 1sc in each sc to end.
Row 15: Ch1, 1sc in same sc, 1sc in each sc to end. (*9 sts*)
Fasten off.

EYE SURROUNDS
(make 2)
Round 1: Using B, ch4, join with a sl st to form a ring.
Round 2: Ch1 (counts as first sc), 7sc in ring, join with a sl st. (*8 sts*)
Fasten off.

TONGUE
Row 1: Using D, ch5.
Row 2: 1sc in 2nd ch from hook (missed ch does not count as sc), 1sc in each ch to end. (*4 sts*)
Rows 3–5: Ch1 (counts as first sc), 1sc in next sc, 1sc in each sc to end.
Fasten off.

TO MAKE UP
Place the front and with back with right sides together. Using A, work a single crochet seam around (see page 140), leaving an opening of approx. 6in (15cm). Turn right side out.

Using E, sew the nose markings onto the snout (see page 141). Insert the safety nose using the photo as a guide and secure with the back (see page 141). Stuff and sew to the front of the pillow. Sew the jowls around the top and sides of the snout.

Add the eyes to the eye surrounds and secure with the backs. Sew the eye surrounds above the snout using the photo as a guide for position. Insert the pillow form and then sew the opening closed.

Take two ear pieces and place wrong sides together. Using B, work one round of single crochet evenly around outer edge, working through both layers to join both pieces together and working 2sc in same place at each corner. Fasten off and then sew the ears on either side at the top of the head.

ADDING FUR
Adding the fur on the face can be done in two ways, either with a crochet hook (see page 141) or threading each strand through with a yarn needle and then tying the ends in a knot close to the fabric. The needle is better for getting in small areas, such as around the eyes.

Face
Cut lengths of A, B, and C approx. 5in (12.5cm) long. The fur can be added with the three colors mixed to suit your design or to resemble a particular dog. Start by working at the base of the pillow right across the front, filling in any gaps and working upward in rows approx. 1in (2.5cm) apart. The closer you put the lines of fur fringe, the fluffier it will be when brushed. Continue to add lines of fur fringing above the snout and all around the face, changing the shades of yarn as required. Brush with a stiff brush or pet brush to give the fluffy look. Trim to shape and length required.

To hold the fur in place it may be beneficial to spray lightly with hairspray (optional).

chocolate labrador pillow

The Labrador Retriever has been a beloved companion for many years, so why not have your pet's happy face crocheted in a pillow that will sit on any couch or bed? Worked in simple single and double crochet stitches throughout, this pillow is an easy make.

SKILL RATING ●○○

YARN AND MATERIALS
King Cole Big Value Super Chunky (100% acrylic), super bulky (super chunky) weight yarn, 90yd (81m) per 3½oz (100g) ball
  4 balls of Brown 31 (A)
Small amount of black light worsted (DK) weight yarn (B)
1 3/16in (30mm) safety nose
Small amount of toy fiberfill
Pair of 1in (24mm) safety eyes
14in (35.5cm) pillow form
Hairspray (optional)

HOOK AND EQUIPMENT
US J-10 (6mm) crochet hook
Stitch marker
Yarn needle
Stiff brush or pet brush

FINISHED SIZE
Approx. 15in (38cm) diameter

ABBREVIATIONS
See page 142.

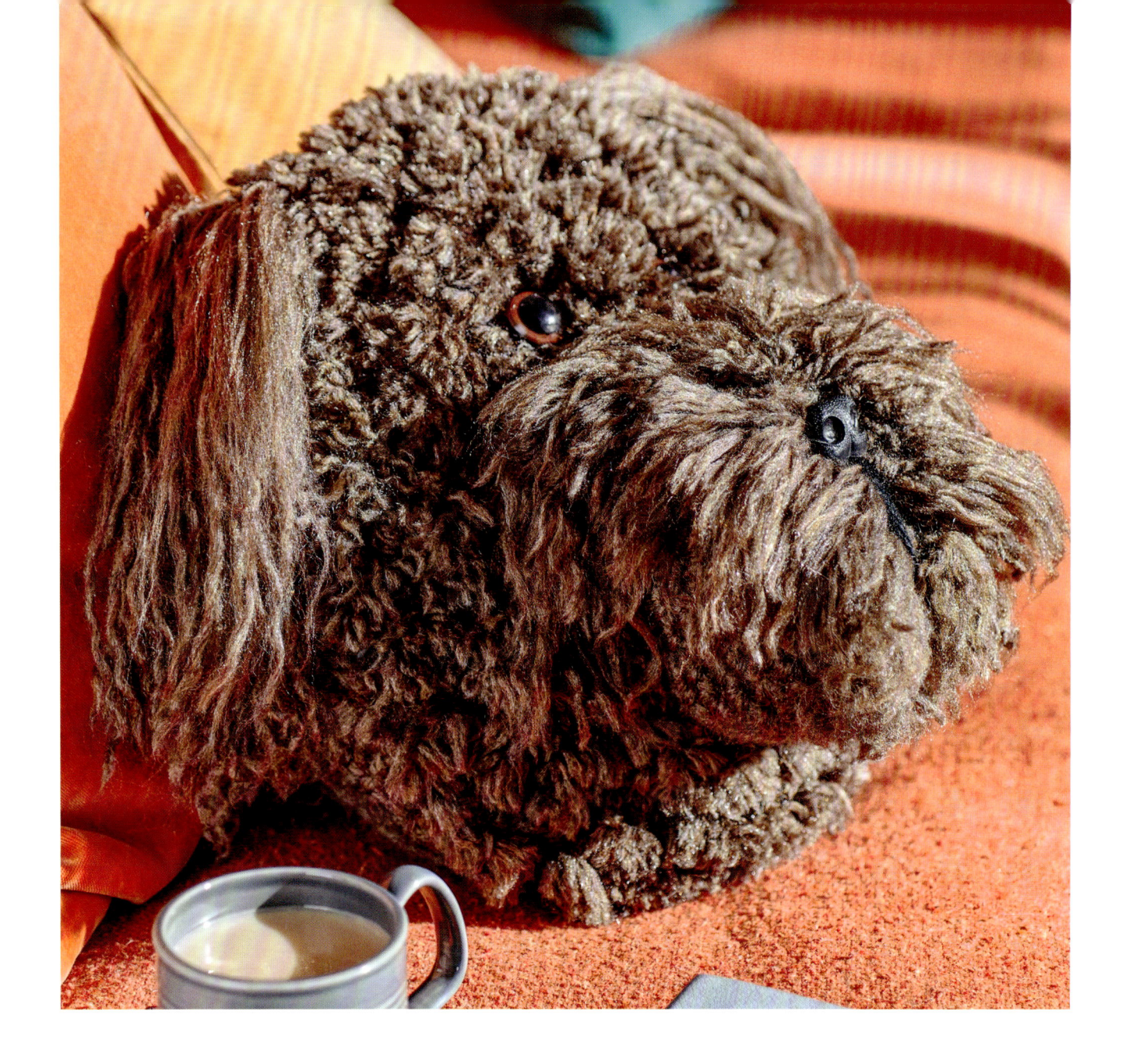

PILLOW FRONT AND BACK
(make 2)
Round 1: Using A, ch4, join with a sl st to form a ring.
Round 2: Ch3 (counts as first dc), 11dc in ring, join with a sl st. (*12 sts*)
Round 3: Ch3, 1dc in same dc, [2dc in next dc] to end, join with a sl st. (*24 sts*)
Round 4: Ch3, 2dc in next dc, [1dc in next dc, 2dc in next dc] to end, join with a sl st. (*36 sts*)
Round 5: Ch3, 1dc in next dc, 2dc in next dc, [1dc in each of next 2 dc, 2dc in next dc] to end, join with a sl st. (*48 sts*)
Round 6: Ch3, 1dc in each of next 2 dc, 2dc in next dc, [1dc in each of next 3 dc, 2dc in next dc] to end, join with a sl st. (*60 sts*)
Round 7: Ch3, 1dc in each of next 3 dc, 2dc in next dc, [1dc in each of next 4 dc, 2dc in next dc] to end, join with a sl st. (*72 sts*)
Round 8: Ch3, 1dc in each of next 4 dc, 2dc in next dc, [1dc in each of next 5 dc, 2dc in next dc] to end, join with a sl st. (*84 sts*)
Round 9: Ch3, 1dcBLO in next dc, 1dcBLO in each dc to end, join with a sl st.
Fasten off.

SNOUT
Round 1: Using A, ch4, join with a sl st to form a ring.
Round 2: Ch1 (counts as first sc), 7sc in ring, join with a sl st. (*8 sts*)

Round 3: Ch1, 2sc in next sc, [1sc in next sc, 2sc in next sc] to end, join with a sl st. (*12 sts*)
Round 4: Ch1, 1sc in next sc, 2sc in next sc, [1sc in each of next 2 sc, 2sc in next sc] to end, join with a sl st. (*16 sts*)
Round 5: Ch1, 1sc in each of next 2 sc, 2sc in next sc, [1sc in each of next 3 sc, 2sc in next sc] to end, join with a sl st. (*20 sts*)
Round 6: Ch1, 1sc in next sc, 1sc in each sc to end, join with a sl st.
Round 7: Ch1, 1sc in each of next 3 sc, 2sc in next sc, [1sc in each of next 4 sc, 2sc in next sc] to end, join with a sl st. (*24 sts*)
Round 8: Ch1, 1sc in each of next 4 sc, 2sc in next sc, [1sc in each of next 5 sc, 2sc in next sc] to end, join with a sl st. (*28 sts*)
Rounds 9–12: Ch1, 1sc in next sc, 1sc in each sc to end, join with a sl st.
Fasten off.

TO MAKE UP
Place the front and back with right sides together and work a single crochet seam around (see page 140), leaving an opening of approx. 6in (15cm). Turn right side out.

Using B, sew the nose markings onto the snout (see page 141), using the photo as a guide. Insert the safety nose and secure with the back. Stuff the snout firmly and sew to the front of the pillow in the position required.

Add the eyes above the snout and secure with the backs through the gap in the pillow (see page 141). Insert the pillow form, and then sew the opening closed. Sew in any loose ends (see page 139).

ADDING FUR
Adding the fur on the face can be done in two ways, either with a crochet hook (see page 141) or threading each strand through with a yarn needle and then tying the ends in a knot close to the fabric. The needle is better for getting into small areas, such as around the eyes.

Ears
Cut lengths of A approx. 10in (25.5cm) long. Starting on one side of head, work a line of fur fringing to form the ear for approx. 2in (5cm) across the pillow. Repeat on the other side. Brush with a stiff brush or pet brush to give the fluffy look and trim to length required.

Snout fur
Cut lengths of A approx. 5in (12.5cm) long. Starting at the middle work a line of fur in the stitches along the top of the snout. Repeat on the other side. Brush for the fluffy effect and trim close to the snout to the length required.

Lower face fur
Continue with the 5in (12.5cm) lengths to cover the bottom of the face and under the snout. Brush and trim to approx. 1in (2.5cm) in line with the bottom of the pillow. This will give the short-cropped fur effect that is needed.

Rest of the face
Cut lengths of A approx. 5in (12.5cm) long. Continue to add lines of fur around the rest of the face. Brush and trim to approx. 1in (2.5cm) to just cover the face with short close-cropped fur. Fasten off all ends (see page 139).

It may be beneficial to spray with hairspray to keep the yarn in place (optional).

This charming pillow mimics the cheeky little face of the popular and lively French Bulldog and almost says "bonjour." It's worked in super bulky yarn and very easy to match to your own dog just by changing the shades of yarn.

french bulldog pillow

PILLOW FRONT AND BACK
(make 2)
Round 1: Using A, ch4, join with a sl st to form a ring.
Round 2: Ch3 (counts as first dc), 11dc in ring, join with a sl st. (*12 sts*)
Round 3: Ch3, 1dc in same dc, [2dc in next dc] to end, join with a sl st. (*24 sts*)
Round 4: Ch3, 2dc in next dc, [1dc in next dc, 2dc in next dc] to end, join with a sl st. (*36 sts*)
Round 5: Ch3, 1dc in next dc, 2dc in next dc, [1dc in each of next 2 dc, 2dc in next dc] to end, join with a sl st. (*48 sts*)
Round 6: Ch3, 1dc in each of next 2 dc, 2dc in next dc, [1dc in each of next 3 dc, 2dc in next dc] to end, join with a sl st. (*60 sts*)
Round 7: Ch3, 1dc in each of next 3 dc, 2dc in next dc, [1dc in each of next 4 dc, 2dc in next dc] to end, join with a sl st. (*72 sts*)
Round 8: Ch3, 1dc in each of next 4 dc, 2dc in next dc, [1dc in each of next 5 dc, 2dc in next dc] to end, join with a sl st. (*84 sts*)
Round 9: Ch3, 1dc in each of next 5 dc, 2dc in next dc, [1dc in each of next 6 dc, 2dc in next dc] to end, join with a sl st. (*96 sts*)
Fasten off.

JOWLS FOR ABOVE SNOUT
Row 1: Using A, ch16.
Row 2: 1sc in 2nd ch from hook (missed ch does not count as sc), 1sc in each ch to end. (*15 sts*)
Rows 3–20: Ch1 (counts as first sc), 1sc in next sc, 1sc in each sc to end.
Fasten off.
Fold in half widthwise and sew together along bottom.

End of jowl
Row 1: At one end, join A and work 6sc evenly, working through both thicknesses to crochet together. (*6 sts*)
Row 2: Sc2tog, 1sc in each of next 2 sc, sc2tog. (*4 sts*)
Row 3: [Sc2tog] twice. (*2 sts*)
Fasten off.
Work end of jowl on other side.

SKILL RATING ● ● ○

YARN AND MATERIALS
King Cole Big Value Super Chunky (100% acrylic), super bulky (super chunky) weight yarn, 90yd (81m) per 3½oz (100g) ball
  5 balls of Graphite 1545
  (dark gray) (A)
  Small amount of Black 8 (B)
1³⁄₁₆in (30mm) safety nose
Small amount of toy fiberfill
Pair of 1in (24mm) safety eyes
14in (35.5cm) diameter pillow form

HOOK AND EQUIPMENT
US J-10 (6mm) crochet hook
Stitch marker
Yarn needle
Stiff brush or pet brush

FINISHED SIZE
Approx. 15in (38cm) diameter

ABBREVIATIONS
See page 142.

SNOUT
Round 1: Using A, ch4, join with a sl st to form a ring.
Round 2: Ch1 (counts as first sc), 7sc in ring, join with a sl st. (*8 sts*)
Round 3: Ch1, 2sc in next sc, [1sc in next sc, 2sc in next sc] to end, join with a sl st. (*12 sts*)
Round 4: Ch1, 1sc in next sc, 2sc in next sc, [1sc in each of next 2 sc, 2sc in next sc] to end, join with a sl st. (*16 sts*)
Round 5: Ch1, 1sc in next sc, 1sc in each sc to end, join with a sl st.
Round 6: Ch1, 1sc in each of next 2 sc, 2sc in next sc, [1sc in each of next 3 sc, 2sc in next sc] to end, join with a sl st. (*20 sts*)
Rounds 7 and 8: Ch1, 1sc in next sc, 1sc in each sc to end, join with a sl st.
Fasten off.

french bulldog pillow

Round 11: Ch1, 1sc in each of next 3 sc, sc2tog, [1sc in each of next 4 sc, sc2tog] to end, join with a sl st. (*20 sts*)
Round 12: Ch1, 1sc in each of next 2 sc, sc2tog, [1sc in each of next 3 sc, sc2tog] to end, join with a sl st. (*16 sts*)
Rounds 13 and 14: Ch1, 1sc in next sc, 1sc in each sc to end, join with a sl st.
Fold flat and work one row of sc across opening, working through both layers across bottom of ear to join.
Fasten off, leaving a length of yarn.

TO MAKE UP
Place the front and back with right sides together and work a single crochet seam around (see page 140), leaving an opening of approx. 6in (15cm). Turn right side out.

Using B, sew the nose markings onto the snout using the photo as a guide (see page 141). Insert the safety nose in the position required and secure with the back (see page 141). Stuff and sew to the front of the pillow using the photo as a guide. Sew the jowls on top of the snout and add the eyes above the snout, securing with the backs through the opening in the pillow.

Insert the pillow form, and then sew the opening closed.

Sew the ears to the head using the photo as a guide for position. Sew in any loose ends (see page 139).

ADDING FUR
Adding the fur on the face can be done in two ways, either with a crochet hook (see page 141) or threading each strand through with a yarn needle and then tying the ends in a knot close to the fabric. The needle is better for getting in small areas, such as around the eyes.

Face
Cut lengths of A approx. 5in (12.5cm) long. Starting at top side of the head, work a line of fur fringing along the top of the forehead. Work more lines approx. 1in (2.5cm) apart until the whole face is covered. Brush with a stiff brush or pet brush to give the fluffy effect and then trim to give the short fur look.

EARS
(make 2)
Round 1: Using A, ch4, join with a sl st to form a ring.
Round 2: Ch1 (counts as first sc), 7sc in ring, join with a sl st. (*8 sts*)
Round 3: Ch1, 2sc in next sc, [1sc in next sc, 2sc in next sc] to end, join with a sl st. (*12 sts*)
Round 4: Ch1, 1sc in next sc, 1sc in each sc to end, join with a sl st.
Round 5: Ch1, 1sc in next sc, 2sc in next sc, [1sc in each of next 2 sc, 2sc in next sc] to end, join with a sl st. (*16 sts*)
Round 6: Ch1, 1sc in next sc, 1sc in each sc to end, join with a sl st.
Round 7: Ch1, 1sc in each of next 2 sc, 2sc in next sc, [1sc in each of next 3 sc, 2sc in next sc] to end, join with a sl st. (*20 sts*)
Round 8: Ch1, 1sc in next sc, 1sc in each sc to end, join with a sl st.
Round 9: Ch1, 1sc in each of next 3 sc, 2sc in next sc, [1sc in each of next 4 sc, 2sc in next sc] to end, join with a sl st. (*24 sts*)
Round 10: Ch1, 1sc in next sc, 1sc in each sc to end, join with a sl st.

poodle pillow

A regal looking Poodle will grace any couch or chair with its loveable face. This very popular breed is seen in many shades, so it's easy to make it resemble a favorite pet. The pillow is made with crocheted rounds of double crochet stitches with the fur added in different lengths as required.

SKILL RATING ● ● ○

YARN AND MATERIALS
King Cole Big Value Super Chunky (100% acrylic), super bulky (super chunky) weight yarn, 90yd (81m) per 3½oz (100g) ball
  4 balls of Latte 3490 (light brown) (A)

Small amount of black light worsted (DK) weight yarn (B)

1 3/16in (30mm) safety nose

Small amount of toy fiberfill

Pair of 1in (24mm) safety eyes

14in (35.5cm) diameter pillow form
Hairspray (optional)

HOOK AND EQUIPMENT
US J-10 (6mm) crochet hook
Stitch marker
Yarn needle
Stiff brush or pet brush

FINISHED SIZE
Approx. 15in (38cm) in diameter

ABBREVIATIONS
See page 142.

PILLOW FRONT AND BACK
(make 2)
Round 1: Using A, ch4, join with a sl st to form a ring.
Round 2: Ch3 (counts as first dc), 11dc in ring, join with a sl st. (*12 sts*)
Round 3: Ch3, 1dc in same dc, [2dc in next dc] to end, join with a sl st. (*24 sts*)
Round 4: Ch3, 2dc in next dc, [1dc in next dc, 2dc in next dc] to end, join with a sl st. (*36 sts*)
Round 5: Ch3, 1dc in next dc, 2dc in next dc, [1dc in each of next 2 dc, 2dc in next dc] to end, join with a sl st. (*48 sts*)
Round 6: Ch3, 1dc in each of next 2 dc, 2dc in next dc, [1dc in each of next 3 dc, 2dc in next dc] to end, join with a sl st. (*60 sts*)
Round 7: Ch3, 1dc in each of next 3 dc, 2dc in next dc, [1dc in each of next 4 dc, 2dc in next dc] to end, join with a sl st. (*72 sts*)
Round 8: Ch3, 1dc in each of next 4 dc, 2dc in next dc, [1dc in each of next 5 dc, 2dc in next dc] to end, join with a sl st. (*84 sts*)
Round 9: Ch3, 1dc in each of next 5 dc, 2dc in next dc, [1dc in each of next 6 dc, 2dc in next dc] to end, join with a sl st. (*96 sts*)
Fasten off.

SNOUT
Round 1: Using A, ch4, join with a sl st to form a ring.
Round 2: Ch1 (counts as first sc), 7sc in ring, join with a sl st. (*8 sts*)
Round 3: Ch1, 1sc in same sc, [2sc in next sc] to end, join with a sl st. (*16 sts*)
Round 4: Ch1, 1sc in next sc, 1sc in each sc to end, join with a sl st.
Round 5: Ch1, 2sc in next sc, [1sc in next sc, 2sc in next sc] to end, join with a sl st. (*24 sts*)
Rounds 6–12: Ch1, 1sc in next sc, 1sc in each sc to end, join with a sl st.
Fasten off.

EARS
(make 2)
Round 1: Using A, ch4, join with a sl st to form a ring.
Round 2: Ch1 (counts as first sc), 7sc in ring, join with a sl st. (*8 sts*)
Round 3: Ch1, 1sc in next sc, 1sc in each sc to end, join with a sl st.
Round 4: Ch1, 2sc in next sc, [1sc in next sc, 2sc in next sc] to end, join with a sl st. (*12 sts*)
Round 5: Ch1, 1sc in next sc, 1sc in each sc to end, join with a sl st.
Round 6: Ch1, 1sc in next sc, 2sc in next sc, [1sc in each of next 2 sc, 2sc in next sc] to end, join with a sl st. (*16 sts*)
Rounds 7–13: Ch1, 1sc in next sc, 1sc in each sc to end, join with a sl st.
Round 14: Ch1, 1sc in next sc, sc2tog, [1sc in each of next 2 sc, sc2tog] to end, join with a sl st. (*12 sts*)
Round 15: Ch1, sc2tog, [1sc in next sc, sc2tog] to end, join with a sl st. (*8 sts*)
Fasten off.

TO MAKE UP
Place the front and back with right sides together. Using A, work a single crochet seam around (see page 140), leaving an opening of approx. 6in (15cm). Turn right side out.

Using B, embroider the nose and mouth markings on the snout (see page 141). Add the safety nose and secure with the back (see page 141). Stuff the snout lightly and sew to front of pillow.

Add the safety eyes above the snout and secure with the backs through the opening in the seam. Insert the pillow form, and then sew the opening closed.

Fold each ear flat and sew the opening closed. Sew the ears on either side of the head. Sew in any loose ends (see page 139).

ADDING FUR
Adding the fur on the face can be done in two ways, either with a crochet hook (see page 141) or threading each strand through with a yarn needle and then tying the ends in a knot close to the fabric. The needle is better for getting in small areas, such as around the eyes.

Snout
Cut A into 6in (15cm) lengths. Start by working lines of fur fringing around the base of the snout. As you work, brush with a stiff brush or pet brush to give the fluffy look and trim to length required—for the lower part of the face and eye area the fur is shorter.

Rest of face
Continue to add lines of fur fringing all around the front of the pillow until you reach just past the eye line. For the area above the eyes continue to add the lines of fur but keep them closer together. Brush with a stiff brush or pet brush to give the fluffy look and trim to a longer length here.

Ears
Add a row of fur fringing on the ears approx. 1in (2.5cm) from the bottom and then brush. Add more lines approx. 1in (2.5cm) apart until you reach the top of the ear. Brush to give the fluffy effect and trim to shape.

It may be beneficial to spray with hairspray to keep the yarn in place (optional).

poodle pillow

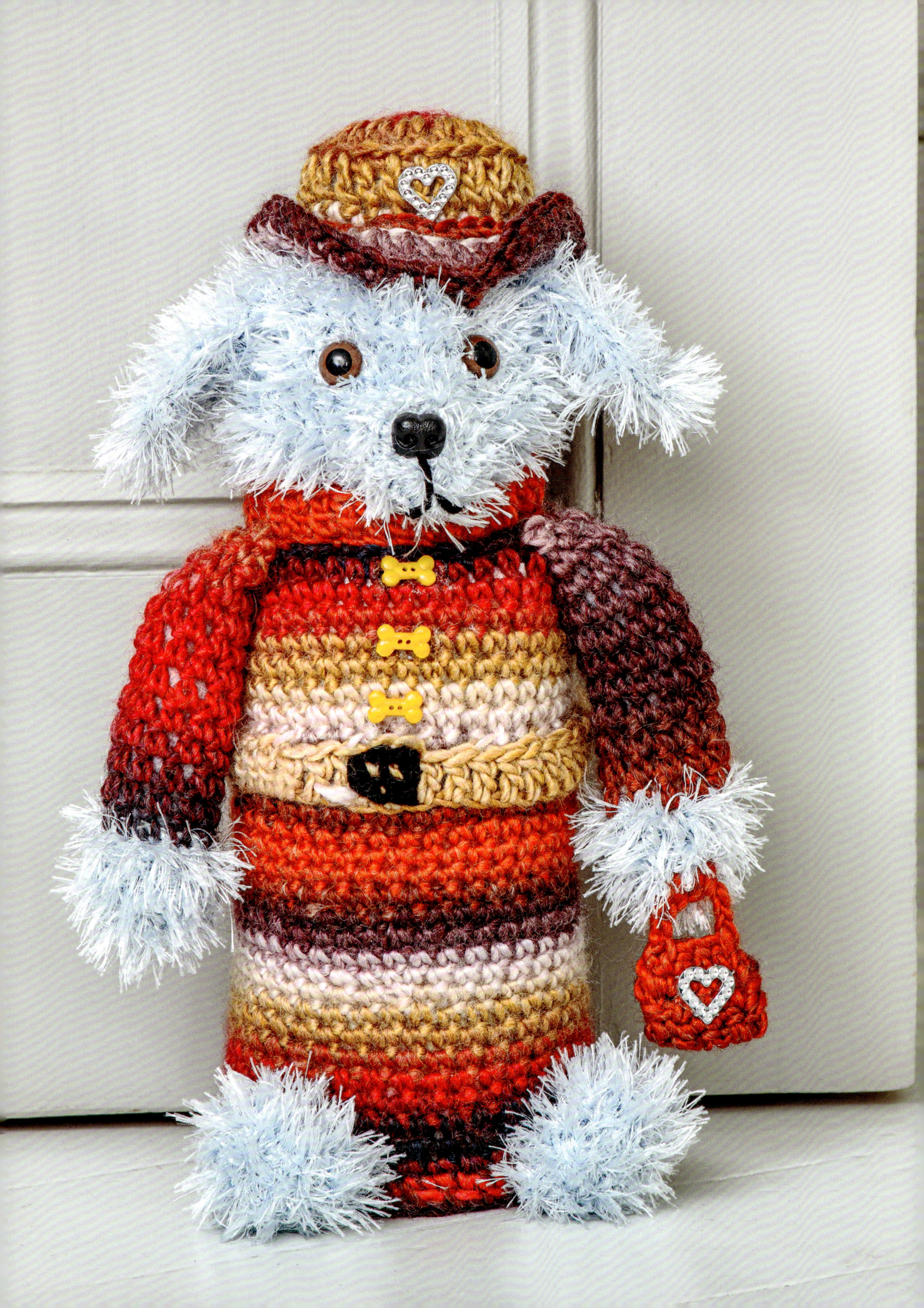

CHAPTER 2
home décor

Created in single crochet stitches throughout, the body of the adult Dachshund is crocheted in one piece, making this a great project for the beginner.

dachshund draft excluder

SKILL RATING ● ○ ○

YARN AND MATERIALS
King Cole Big Value Super Chunky (100% acrylic), super bulky (super chunky) weight yarn, 90yd (81m) per 3½oz (100g) ball
  5 balls of Brass 3400 (orange brown) (A)

King Cole Big Value Chunky (100% acrylic), bulky (chunky) weight yarn, 167yd (152m) per 3½oz (100g) ball
  1 ball of Blue Heaven 559 (blue) (B)
  1 ball of Turmeric 3486 (orange brown) (C)

Small amount of black light worsted (DK) weight yarn (D)

¾in (18mm) safety nose

Toy fiberfill

Pair of ⅝in (15mm) safety eyes

Embellishments of your choice

HOOKS AND EQUIPMENT
US 7 (4.5mm) and US I-9 (5.5mm) crochet hooks

Stitch marker

Yarn needle

FINISHED SIZE
Approx. 40in (101cm) long, 16in (41cm) diameter

ABBREVIATIONS
See page 142.

PATTERN NOTE
If the draft excluder will be within reach of a young child, substitute the embellishments and the safety nose and eyes with embroidery in yarn (see page 141).

ADULT DOG
BODY
Round 1: Using A and US I-9 (5.5mm) hook, ch4, join with a sl st to form a ring.
Round 2: Ch1 (counts as first sc), 7sc in ring, join with a sl st. (*8 sts*)
Round 3: Ch1, 1sc in same sc, [2sc in next sc] to end, join with a sl st. (*16 sts*)

Round 4: Ch1, 2sc in next sc, [1sc in next sc, 2sc in next sc] to end, join with a sl st. (*24 sts*)
Round 5: Ch1, 1sc in next sc, 2sc in next sc, [1sc in each of next 2 sc, 2sc in next sc] to end, join with a sl st. (*32 sts*)
Round 6: Ch1, 1sc in each of next 2 sc, 2sc in next sc, [1sc in each of next 3 sc, 2sc in next sc] to end, join with a sl st. (*40 sts*)
Round 7: Ch1, 1scBLO in next sc, 1scBLO in each sc to end, join with a sl st.
Rounds 8–90: Ch1, 1sc in next sc, 1sc in each sc to end, join with a sl st.
Round 91: Working in BLO, ch1, 1sc in each of next 2 sc, sc2tog, [1sc in each of next 3 sc, sc2tog] to end, join with a sl st. (*32 sts*)
Round 92: Ch1, 1sc in next sc, sc2tog, [1sc in each of next 2 sc, sc2tog] to end, join with a sl st. (*24 sts*)
Round 93: Ch1, sc2tog, [1sc in next sc, sc2tog] to end, join with a sl st. (*16 sts*)
Stuff body firmly.
Round 94: [Sc2tog] to end, join with a sl st. (*8 sts*)
Fasten off, leaving a length of yarn.
Thread end onto needle, gather remaining sts together. Fasten off.

HEAD
Round 1: Using A and US I-9 (5.5mm) hook, ch4, join with a sl st to form a ring.

Round 2: Ch1 (counts as first sc), 7sc in ring, join with a sl st. (*8 sts*)
Round 3: Ch1, 2sc in next sc, [1sc in next sc, 2sc in next sc] to end, join with a sl st. (*12 sts*)
Rounds 4 and 5: Ch1, 1sc in next sc, 1sc in each sc to end, join with a sl st.
Round 6: Ch1, 1sc in next sc, 2sc in next sc, [1sc in each of next 2 sc, 2sc in next sc] to end, join with a sl st. (*16 sts*)
Round 7: Ch1, 1sc in next sc, 1sc in each sc to end, join with a sl st.
Round 8: Ch1, 1sc in each of next 2 sc, 2sc in next sc, [1sc in each of next 3 sc, 2sc in next sc] to end, join with a sl st. (*20 sts*)
Round 9: Ch1, 1sc in next sc, 1sc in each sc to end, join with a sl st.
Round 10: Ch1, 1sc in each of next 3 sc, 2sc in next sc, [1sc in each of next 4 sc, 2sc in next sc] to end, join with a sl st. (*24 sts*)
Round 11: Ch1, 2sc in next sc, [1sc in next sc, 2sc in next sc] to end, join with a sl st. (*36 sts*)
Round 12: Ch1, 1sc in next sc, 1sc in each sc to end, join with a sl st.
Round 13: Ch1, 1sc in each of next 4 sc, 2sc in next sc, [1sc in each of next 5 sc, 2sc in next sc] to end, join with a sl st. (*42 sts*)
Rounds 14–18: Ch1, 1sc in next sc, 1sc in each sc to end, join with a sl st.

Row 16: Sc2tog, 1sc in each sc to last 2 sc, sc2tog. (*7 sts*)
Fasten off.

LEGS
(make 4)
Round 1: Using A and US I-9 (5.5mm) hook, ch4, join with a sl st to form a ring.
Round 2: Ch1 (counts as first sc), 7sc in ring, join with a sl st. (*8 sts*)
Round 3: Ch1, 1sc in next sc, 1sc in each sc to end, join with a sl st.
Round 4: Ch1, 2sc in next sc, [1sc in next sc, 2sc in next sc] to end, join with a sl st. (*12 sts*)
Rounds 5–10: Ch1, 1sc in next sc, 1sc in each sc to end, join with a sl st.
Fasten off.

TAIL
Row 1: Using A and US I-9 (5.5mm) hook, ch3.
Row 2: 1sc in 2nd ch from hook (missed ch does not count as sc), 1sc in next ch. (*2 sts*)
Row 3: Ch1 (counts as first sc), 1sc in same sc, 1sc in each sc to end. (*3 sts*)
Row 4: Ch1, 1sc in same sc, 1sc in each sc to end. (*4 sts*)
Row 5: Ch1, 1sc in same sc, 1sc in each sc to end. (*5 sts*)
Row 6: Ch1, 1sc in same sc, 1sc in each sc to end. (*6 sts*)
Row 7: Ch1, 1sc in same sc, 1sc in each sc to end. (*7 sts*)
Row 8: Ch1, 1sc in same sc, 1sc in each sc to end. (*8 sts*)
Row 9: Ch1, 1sc in same sc, 1sc in each sc to end. (*9 sts*)
Rows 10–13: Ch1, 1sc in next sc, 1sc in each sc to end.
Fasten off.

ADULT DOG COLLAR
Row 1: Using B and US 7 (4.5mm) hook, ch30.
Row 2: 1dc in 3rd ch from hook (missed 2 ch do not count as dc), 1dc in each ch to end. (*28 sts*)
Fasten off.

ADULT DOG COAT
Row 1: Using B and US 7 (4.5mm) hook, ch43.
Row 2: 1sc in 2nd ch from hook (missed ch does not count as sc), 1sc in each ch to end. (*42 sts*)
Rows 3–62: Ch1 (counts as first sc), 1sc in next sc, 1sc in each sc to end.
Fasten off.

Round 19: Ch1, 1sc in each of next 4 sc, sc2tog, [1sc in each of next 5 sc, sc2tog] to end, join with a sl st. (*36 sts*)
Round 20: Ch1, sc2tog, [1sc in next sc, sc2tog] to end, join with a sl st. (*24 sts*)
Round 21: Ch1, sc2tog, [1sc in next sc, sc2tog] to end, join with a sl st. (*16 sts*)
Round 22: Ch1, 1sc in next sc, 1sc in each sc to end, join with a sl st.
Round 23: [Sc2tog] to end, join with a sl st. (*8 sts*)
Fasten off, leaving a length of yarn for sewing.

EARS
(make 2)
Row 1: Using A and US I-9 (5.5mm) hook, ch4.
Row 2: 1sc in 2nd ch from hook (missed ch does not count as sc), 1sc in each ch to end. (*3 sts*)
Row 3: Ch1 (counts as first sc), 1sc in same sc, 1sc in each sc to end. (*4 sts*)
Row 4: Ch1, 1sc in same sc, 1sc in each sc to end. (*5 sts*)
Row 5: Ch1, 1sc in same sc, 1sc in each sc to end. (*6 sts*)
Row 6: Ch1, 1sc in same sc, 1sc in each sc to end. (*7 sts*)
Row 7: Ch1, 1sc in same sc, 1sc in each sc to end. (*8 sts*)
Row 8: Ch1, 1sc in same sc, 1sc in each sc to end. (*9 sts*)
Rows 9–15: Ch1, 1sc in next sc, 1sc in each sc to end.

EDGING

Rejoin B in one corner, ch3 (counts as first dc), working along row ends, 1dc in next sc, 1dc in each sc to corner. Fasten off.
Repeat for other edge.

POCKET FOR COAT

Row 1: Using B and US 7 (4.5mm) hook, ch40.
Row 2: 1dc in 3rd ch from hook (missed 2 ch do not count as dc), 1dc in each ch to end. (*38 sts*)
Rows 3 and 4: Ch3 (counts as first dc), 1dc in next dc, 1dc in each dc to end.
Row 5: Ch1 (counts as first sc), 1sc in next dc, 1sc in each dc to end.
Fasten off.

MAIN PUPPY
BODY

Round 1: Using C and US 7 (4.5mm) hook, ch4, join with a sl st to form a ring.
Round 2: Ch1 (counts as first sc), 7sc in ring, join with a sl st. (*8 sts*)
Round 3: Ch1, 2sc in next sc, [1sc in next sc, 2sc in next sc] to end, join with a sl st. (*12 sts*)
Round 4: Ch1, 1sc in next sc, 2sc in next sc, [1sc in each of next 2 sc, 2sc in next sc] to end, join with a sl st. (*16 sts*)
Round 5: Ch1, 1scBLO in next sc, 1scBLO in each sc to end, join with a sl st.
Rounds 6–18: Ch1, 1sc in next sc, 1sc in each sc to end, join with a sl st.
Round 19: Ch1, 1scBLO in next sc, 1scBLO in each sc to end, join with a sl st.
Round 20: Ch1, 1sc in next sc, sc2tog, [1sc in each of next 2 sc, sc2tog] to end, join with a sl st. (*12 sts*)
Stuff body firmly.
Round 21: Ch1, sc2tog, [1sc in next sc, sc2tog] to end, join with a sl st. (*8 sts*)
Fasten off, leaving a length of yarn.
Thread end onto needle, gather remaining sts together. Fasten off.

HEAD

Round 1: Using C and US 7 (4.5mm) hook, ch4, join with a sl st to form a ring.
Round 2: Ch1 (counts as first sc), 7sc in ring, join with a sl st. (*8 sts*)
Round 3: Ch1, 1sc in next sc, 1sc in each sc to end, join with a sl st.
Round 4: Ch1, 2sc in next sc, [1sc in next sc, 2sc in next sc] to end, join with a sl st. (*12 sts*)
Round 5: Ch1, 1sc in next sc, 2sc in next sc, [1sc in each of next 2 sc, 2sc in next sc] to end, join with a sl st. (*16 sts*)
Round 6: Ch1, 1sc in next sc, 1sc in each sc to end, join with a sl st.
Round 7: Ch1, 1sc in next sc, sc2tog, [1sc in each of next 2 sc, sc2tog] to end, join with a sl st. (*12 sts*)
Stuff head firmly.
Round 8: Ch1, sc2tog, [1sc in next sc, sc2tog] to end, join with a sl st. (*8 sts*)
Fasten off, leaving a length of yarn.
Thread end onto needle, gather remaining sts together. Fasten off.

EARS

(make 2)
Row 1: Using C and US 7 (4.5mm) hook, ch3.
Row 2: 1sc in 2nd ch from hook (missed ch does not count as sc), 1sc in next ch. (*2 sts*)
Row 3: Ch1 (counts as first sc), 1sc in same sc, 1sc in each sc to end. (*3 sts*)
Row 4: Ch1, 1sc in same sc, 1sc in each sc to end. (*4 sts*)
Row 5: Ch1, 1sc in same sc, 1sc in each sc to end. (*5 sts*)
Row 6: Sc2tog, 1sc in next sc, sc2tog. (*3 sts*)
Fasten off.

dachshund draft excluder

LEGS
(make 4)
Round 1: Using C and US 7 (4.5mm) hook, ch4, join with a sl st to form a ring.
Round 2: Ch1 (counts as first sc), 5sc in ring, join with a sl st. (*6 sts*)
Rounds 3-6: Ch1, 1sc in next sc, 1sc in each sc to end, join with a sl st.
Fasten off.

MAIN PUPPY COLLAR
Row 1: Using B and US 7 (4.5mm) hook, ch12.
Fasten off.

POCKET PUPPIES
(make 3)
Work head, collar, pair of ears and pair of front legs for each puppy as for main puppy. For body, work as for main puppy body to Round 12. Fasten off.

TO MAKE UP
Adult
Using D, embroider the mouth markings on the head (see page 141) using the photo as a guide. Add the safety nose and secure with the back (see page 141). Add the safety eyes and secure with the safety backs. Stuff the head firmly, then thread the yarn end onto the needle and gather the stitches to close the base. Sew the ears to the head.

Sew the head to the body. Stuff the four legs and sew to the body in suitable positions. Sew tail seam and stuff lightly, then sew the tail to the body.

Wrap the coat around the body in position and sew closed, making sure to keep the seam to the bottom of the dog's body. Sew the pocket across one side of the coat, then sew two seams to make the three pockets.

Main puppy
Using D, embroider the mouth and eyes on the head using the photo as a guide. Sew the ears to the head and then sew the head to the body. Stuff the four legs and sew to body in suitable positions. Sew the tail seam and then sew the tail to the body.

Pocket puppies
Using D, embroider the mouths and eyes on each head using the photo as a guide. Sew a pair of ears to each head.

Stuff each body lightly and sew across the bottom seam. Sew a head to each body. Stuff the front legs and sew a pair to each body.

Slip a puppy into each pocket and secure with a few stitches.

Add embellishments of your choice.

fluffy terrier wall hanging

Brighten up any wall with this soft, furry little fellow crocheted in a luxury fur yarn using single crochet stitch. The main backing square is crocheted in waffle stitch, which is a mixture of regular double crochet and front post double crochet stitches. A small length of dowel rod is inserted in the crocheted sleeve at the top to form the hanging support.

SKILL RATING ● ● ○

YARN AND MATERIALS
King Cole Big Value Super Chunky (100% acrylic), super bulky (super chunky) weight yarn, 90yd (81m) per 3½oz (100g) ball
   2½ balls in Porcelain 3311 (light purple) (A)

King Cole Luxury Fur (90% nylon, 10% polyester), worsted (Aran) weight yarn, 100yd (92m) per 3½oz (100g) ball
   1 ball of Silver Fox 4207 (gray) (C)

Small amount of navy super bulky (super chunky) weight yarn (B)

Small amount of black light worsted (DK) weight yarn (D)

⅞in (22mm) safety nose

Small amount of toy fiberfill

Pair of ⅝in (16mm) safety eyes

Embellishments of your choice

Approx. 17in (43cm) dowel rod

Length of picture hanging wire or cord

HOOKS AND EQUIPMENT
US H-8 (5mm) and US J-10 (6mm) crochet hooks

Stitch marker

Pins

Yarn needle

Stiff brush or pet brush

Hairspray (optional)

FINISHED SIZE
13 x 17in (33 x 43cm) excluding hanging loop

ABBREVIATIONS
See page 142.

PATTERN NOTE
Yarn C is worked using two strands held together throughout. Yarn C pieces are turned to the "wrong side," which is fluffier, after working.

MAIN WALL HANGING

Row 1: Using A and US J-10 (6mm) hook, ch43.
Row 2: 1dc in 3rd ch from hook (missed 2 ch do not count as dc), 1dc in each ch to end. (*41 sts*)
Row 3: Ch3 (counts as first dc), 1dc in next st, [1FPdc in next st, 1dc in each of next 2 sts] to end.
Row 4: Ch3, 1FPdc in next st, 1dc in next st, [1FPdc in each of next 2 sts, 1dc in next st] to last 2 sts, 1FPdc in next st, 1dc in last st.
Rows 5–20: Repeat Rows 3 and 4 until 10 rows of squares have been completed.
Rows 21 and 22: Ch3, 1dc in next dc, 1dc in each dc to end.
Fasten off, leaving a length of yarn for sewing.
Fold Row 22 onto Row 21 and sew to back of wall hanging to form channel for dowel rod.

SIDES AND BOTTOM

Using A and US J-10 (6mm) hook, work one row of sc evenly along each side.
Fasten off.
Using B, work one row of sc along both sides and bottom edge of wall hanging.
Fasten off.

DOG

HEAD
Row 1: Using two strands of C held together and US H-8 (5mm) hook, ch15.
Row 2: 1sc in 2nd ch from hook (missed ch does not count as sc), 1sc in each sc to end. (*14 sts*)
Row 3: Ch1 (counts as first sc), 1sc in next sc, 1sc in each sc to end.
Row 4: Ch1, 1sc in same sc, 1sc in each sc to last st, 2sc in last sc. (*16 sts*)
Row 5: Ch1, 1sc in next sc, 1sc in each sc to end.
Row 6: Ch1, 2sc in next sc, [1sc in next sc, 2sc in next sc] to end. (*24 sts*)
Row 7: Ch1, 1sc in next sc, 1sc in each sc to end.
Row 8: Ch1, 1sc in next sc, 2sc in next sc, [1sc in each of next 2 sc, 2sc in next sc] to end. (*32 sts*)
Rows 9–21: Ch1, 1sc in next sc, 1sc in each sc to end.
Row 22: Sc2tog, 1sc in each sc to last 2 sc, sc2tog. (*30 sts*)
Fasten off.

60 home décor

TOP OF BODY
Row 1: Using two strands of C held together and US H-8 (5mm) hook, ch31.
Row 2: 1sc in 2nd ch from hook (missed ch does not count as sc), 1sc in each sc to end. (*30 sts*)
Rows 3–6: Ch1 (counts as first sc), 1sc in next sc, 1sc in each sc to end.
Row 7: Sc2tog, 1sc in each sc to last 2 sc, sc2tog. (*28 sts*)
Fasten off.

SNOUT
Round 1: Using two strands of C held together and US H-8 (5mm) hook, ch4, join with a sl st to form a ring. (*4 sts*)
Round 2: Ch1 (counts as first sc), 7sc in ring, join with a sl st. (*8 sts*)
Round 3: Ch1, 2sc in next sc, [1sc in next sc, 2sc in next sc] to end, join with a sl st. (*12 sts*)
Round 4: Ch1, 1sc in next sc, 1sc in each sc to end, join with a sl st.
Round 5: Ch1, 1sc in next sc, 2sc in next sc, [1sc in each of next 2 sc, 2sc in next sc] to end, join with a sl st. (*16 sts*)
Round 6: Ch1, 1sc in each of next 2 sc, 2sc in next sc, [1sc in each of next 3 sc, 2sc in next sc] to end, join with a sl st. (*20 sts*)
Rounds 7 and 8: Ch1, 1sc in next sc, 1sc in each sc to end, join with a sl st.
Fasten off.
Turn work inside out so that the "wrong side" is on the outside.

EARS
(make 2)
Round 1: Using two strands of C held together and US H-8 (5mm) hook, ch4, join with a sl st to form a ring.
Round 2: Ch1 (counts as first sc), 7sc in ring, join with a sl st. (*8 sts*)
Round 3: Ch1, 2sc in next sc, [1sc in next sc, 2sc in next sc] to end, join with a sl st. (*12 sts*)
Rounds 4–6: Ch1, 1sc in next sc, 1sc in each sc to end, join with a sl st.
Fasten off.
Turn work inside out so that the "wrong side" is on the outside.
Flatten ear and sew the opening closed.

COLLAR
Row 1: Using B and US J-10 (6mm) hook, ch18.
Row 2: 1dc in 3rd ch from hook (missed 2 ch do not count as dc), 1dc in each ch to end. (*16 sts*)
Fasten off.

TO MAKE UP
Using D, embroider the mouth markings onto the snout in positions required (see page 141), using the photo as a guide. Insert the safety nose and secure with the back (see page 141). Stuff the snout and sew to the head.

Attach the safety eyes and secure with the backs. Pin the head to the center of the main wall hanging, then sew in place to secure. Sew the ears above the head using the photo as a guide. Sew the collar under the head.

Pin the top of body to the main wall hanging, centered under the head, then sew in place to secure. Brush to give the fluffy effect.

It may be beneficial to spray with hairspray to keep the yarn in place (optional).

Decorate with your chosen embellishments.

Slide the dowel rod through the channel at the top of the wall hanging, then tie a length of picture wire at either end to hang.

doggie doorstops

Crocheted in simple single crochet stitch throughout, these pretty little doorstops are real head-turners. Perfect for using up single balls of yarn, you can make them in many different colors. If you omit the base you can use this design to hold two rolls of toilet paper to brighten any bathroom.

SKILL RATING ● ● ●

YARN AND MATERIALS
King Cole Riot Chunky (30% wool, 70% acrylic), bulky (chunky) weight yarn, 147yd (134m) per 3½oz (100g) ball
- 1½ balls of Springtime 3438 (green multicolored) or Firefly 1691 (red multicolored) (A)

King Cole Moments DK (100% polyester), light worsted (DK) weight yarn, 98yd (90m) per 1¾oz (50g) ball
- 1 ball of White 470 or Silver 485 (gray) (B)

Small amount of black light worsted (DK) weight yarn (C)

Toy fiberfill

Small amount of sand or gravel in plastic bag for weight

¾in (18mm) safety nose

Pair of ⅝in (15mm) safety eyes

Embellishments of your choice

HOOK AND EQUIPMENT
US H-8 (5mm) crochet hook

Stitch marker

Yarn needle

FINISHED SIZE
Approx. 14in (36cm) tall

ABBREVIATIONS
See page 142.

PATTERN NOTES
Yarn B is worked with two strands of yarn held together. It is advisable to use a stitch marker and work on the wrong side.
To make as a holder for two rolls of toilet paper, leave the body open at the bottom; omit the base piece and do not add fiberfill or weight.
If the doorstops will be within reach of a young child, substitute the embellishments and the safety nose and eyes with embroidery in yarn (see page 141).

DOGGY DOORSTOP

MAIN BODY
Round 1: Using A, ch6, join with a sl st to form a ring.
Round 2: Ch3 (counts as first dc), 11dc in ring, join with a sl st. (*12 sts*)
Round 3: Ch3, 1dc in same dc, [2dc in next dc] to end, join with a sl st. (*24 sts*)
Round 4: Ch3, 2dc in next dc, [1dc in next dc, 2dc in next dc] to end, join with a sl st. (*36 sts*)
Round 5: Ch1 (counts as first sc), 1sc in each of next 7 dc, 2sc in next dc, [1sc in each of next 8 dc, 2sc in next dc] to end, join with a sl st. (*40 sts*)
Round 6: Ch1, 1scBLO in next sc, 1scBLO in each sc to end, join with a sl st.
Rounds 7–34: Ch1, 1sc in next sc, 1sc in each sc to end, join with a sl st.
Fasten off.

BASE OF DOORSTOP
Round 1: Using A, ch6, join with a sl st to form a ring.
Round 2: Ch3 (counts as first dc), 11dc in ring, join with a sl st. (*12 sts*)
Round 3: Ch3, 1dc in same dc, [2dc in next dc] to end, join with a sl st. (*24 sts*)
Round 4: Ch3, 2dc in next dc, [1dc in next dc, 2dc in next dc] to end, join with a sl st. (*36 sts*)
Fasten off, leaving a length of yarn for sewing to body.

HEAD
Round 1: Using two strands of B held together, ch4, join with a sl st to form a ring.
Round 2: Ch1 (counts as first sc), 7sc in ring, join with a sl st. (*8 sts*)
Round 3: Ch1, 1sc in same sc, [2sc in next sc] to end, join with a sl st. (*16 sts*)
Round 4: Ch1, 2sc in next sc, [1sc in next sc, 2sc in next sc] to end, join with a sl st. (*24 sts*)
Round 5: Ch1, 1sc in next sc, 1sc in each sc to end, join with a sl st.
Round 6: Ch1, 2sc in next sc, [1sc in next sc, 2sc in next sc] to end, join with a sl st. (*36 sts*)
Rounds 7–14: Ch1, 1sc in next sc, 1sc in each sc to end, join with a sl st.
Round 15: Ch1, sc2tog, [1sc in next sc, sc2tog] to end, join with a sl st. (*24 sts*)
Round 16: Ch1, 1sc in next sc, 1sc in each sc to end, join with a sl st.
Round 17: Ch1, sc2tog, [1sc in next sc, sc2tog] to end, join with a sl st. (*16 sts*)
Round 18: Ch1, 1sc in next sc, 1sc in each sc to end, join with a sl st.
Fasten off.

doggie doorstops

SNOUT
Round 1: Using two strands of B held together, ch4, join with a sl st to form a ring.
Round 2: Ch1 (counts as first sc), 7sc in ring, join with a sl st. (*8 sts*)
Round 3: Ch1, 2sc in next sc, [1sc in next sc, 2sc in next sc] to end, join with a sl st. (*12 sts*)
Rounds 4-6: Ch1, 1sc in next sc, 1sc in each sc to end, join with a sl st.
Fasten off.

EARS
(make 2)
Row 1: Using two strands of B held together, ch7.
Row 2: 1sc in 2nd ch from hook (missed ch does not count as sc), 1sc in each ch to end. (*6 sts*)
Rows 3-12: Ch1 (counts as first sc), 1sc in next sc, 1sc in each sc to end, join with a sl st.
Fasten off.

ARMS
(make 2)
Round 1: Using two strands of B held together, ch4, join with a sl st to form a ring.
Round 2: Ch1 (counts as first sc), 7sc in ring, join with a sl st. (*8 sts*)
Round 3: Ch1, 2sc in next sc, [1sc in next sc, 2sc in next sc] to end, join with a sl st. (*12 sts*)
Rounds 4 and 5: Ch1, 1sc in next sc, 1sc in each sc to end, join with a sl st.
Fasten off B, join A.
Round 6: Ch1, 1scBLO in next sc, 1scBLO in each sc to end, join with a sl st.
Rounds 7-16: Ch1, 1sc in next sc, 1sc in each sc to end, join with a sl st.
Fasten off.

FEET
(make 2)
Round 1: Using two strands of B held together, ch4, join with a sl st to form a ring.
Round 2: Ch1 (counts as first sc), 7sc in ring, join with a sl st. (*8 sts*)
Round 3: Ch1, 2sc in next sc, [1sc in next sc, 2sc in next sc] to end, join with a sl st. (*12 sts*)
Rounds 4-7: Ch1, 1sc in next sc, 1sc in each sc to end, join with a sl st.
Fasten off.

COLLAR FOR SWEATER
Row 1: Using A, ch36.
Row 2: 1dc in 3rd ch from hook (missed 2 ch does not count as dc), 1dc in each ch to end. (*34 sts*)
Fasten off, leaving a length of yarn for sewing to neck.

HAT
Round 1: Using A, ch5.
Round 2: Ch3 (counts as first dc), 11dc in ring, join with a sl st. (*12 sts*)
Round 3: Ch3, 1dc in same dc, [2dc in next dc] to end, join with a sl st. (*24 sts*)
Round 4: Ch3, 1dcBLO in next dc, 1dcBLO in each dc to end, join with a sl st.
Round 5: Ch3, 1dc in next dc, 1dc in each dc to end, join with a sl st.
Round 6: Ch3, 1dcBLO in same dc, [2dcBLO in next dc] to end, join with a sl st. (*48 sts*)
Round 7: Ch1 (counts as first sc), 1sc in next dc, 1sc in each dc to end, join with a sl st.
Fasten off.

BRAID FOR HAT
Using A, wind off a section of yarn in contrasting shade to hat.
Row 1: Ch31.
Row 2: 1sc in 2nd ch from hook (missed ch does not count as sc), 1sc in each ch to end. (*30 sts*)
Fasten off.

64 home décor

BELT
Using A, wind off a section of yarn in contrasting shade to hat.
Row 1: Ch42.
Row 2: 1dc in 3rd ch from hook (missed 2 ch does not count as dc), 1dc in each ch to end. (*40 sts*)
Fasten off.

PURSE
Row 1: Using A, ch6.
Row 2: 1sc in 2nd ch from hook (missed ch does not count as sc), 1sc in each ch to end. (*5 sts*)
Rows 3–10: Ch1 (counts as first sc), 1sc in next sc, 1sc in each sc to end.
Ch8 for handle.
Fasten off.

TO MAKE UP
Stuff the main body firmly, leaving a gap at the bottom. Add the sand or gravel wrapped securely in plastic, then add further fiberfill if required. Sew the base to the bottom.

Head
Using C, sew the mouth markings onto the snout (see page 141). Add the safety nose using the photo as a guide for position and secure with the back (see page 141). Stuff the snout lightly and sew to the head in the position required. Add the safety eyes in the positions required and secure with the backs. Stuff the head. Sew the ears to the head in the positions required, then sew the head to the top of the body.

Stuff the arms lightly and sew to the body in the positions required. Stuff the feet and sew to the base of the doorstop.

Sew the collar around the neck of the sweater. Stuff and sew the hat to the head, then sew the braid around the hat above the brim. Sew the belt around the body. Using C, embroider the buckle onto the belt.

Purse
Fold the bag in half and sew the seam on both sides, leaving the gap open at top. Sew the end of the chain to the other side at the top of the bag to form the handle. Sew the handle of the purse to one paw.

Add any embellishments as required and sew in any loose ends (see page 139).

Crocheted in a very soft furry yarn in single crochet stitch throughout, this cute and furry little character would add a burst of personality to any wall.

fluffy dog framed wall hanging

SKILL RATING ● ● ○

YARN AND MATERIALS
King Cole Baby Alpaca DK (100% baby alpaca) light worsted (DK) weight yarn, 110yd (100m) per 1¾oz (50g) ball
  3 balls of Glacier 3069 (gray) (A)

Small amount of contrast light worsted (DK) weight yarn (B)

Small amount of black light worsted (DK) weight yarn (C)

Toy fiberfill

Pair of ¾in (18mm) safety eyes

10 x 7in (25 x 18cm) photograph frame with glass removed

Fabric glue

Collar embellishment of your choice (optional)

HOOK AND EQUIPMENT
US H-8 (5mm) crochet hook

Stitch marker

Yarn needle

Stiff brush or pet brush

FINISHED SIZE
Approx. 11 x 7in (28 x 18cm)

ABBREVIATIONS
See page 142.

PATTERN NOTES
Yarn A is worked with two strands of yarn held together to give the fluffy effect. It is advisable to use a stitch marker.

DOG
BODY
Round 1: Using two strands of A held together, ch4, join with a sl st to form a ring.
Round 2: Ch1 (counts as first sc), 7sc in ring, join with a sl st. (*8 sts*)
Round 3: Ch1, 1sc in same sc, [2sc in next sc] to end, join with a sl st. (*16 sts*)
Round 4: Ch1, 2sc in next sc, [1sc in next sc, 2sc in next sc] to end, join with a sl st. (*24 sts*)
Round 5: Ch1, 1sc in same sc, [2sc in next sc] twice, 1sc in each of next 9 sc, [2sc in next sc] three times, 1sc in each of next 9 sc, join with a sl st. (*30 sts*)
Rounds 6–10: Ch1, 1sc in next sc, 1sc in each sc to end, join with a sl st.
Fasten off.

HEAD
Round 1: Using two strands of A held together, ch4, join with a sl st to form a ring.
Round 2: Ch1 (counts as first sc), 7sc in ring, join with a sl st. (*8 sts*)
Round 3: Ch1, 1sc in same sc, [2sc in next sc] to end, join with a sl st. (*16 sts*)
Round 4: Ch1, 2sc in next sc, [1sc in next sc, 2sc in next sc] to end, join with a sl st. (*24 sts*)
Round 5: Ch1, 1sc in same sc, [2sc in next sc] twice, 1sc in each of next 9 sc, [2sc in next sc] three times, 1sc in each of next 9 sc, join with a sl st. (*30 sts*)
Round 6: Ch1, 1sc in same sc, [2sc in next sc] twice, 1sc in each of next 12 sc, [2sc in next sc] three times, 1sc in each of next 12 sc, join with a sl st. (*36 sts*)
Round 7: Ch1, 1sc in same sc, 2sc in next sc, 1sc in each of next 16 sc, [2sc in next sc] twice, 1sc in each of next 16 sc, join with a sl st. (*40 sts*)
Rounds 8–14: Ch1, 1sc in next sc, 1sc in each sc to end, join with a sl st.
Round 15: Ch1, 1sc in next sc, sc2tog, [1sc in each of next 2 sc, sc2tog] to end, join with a sl st. (*30 sts*)
Fasten off.

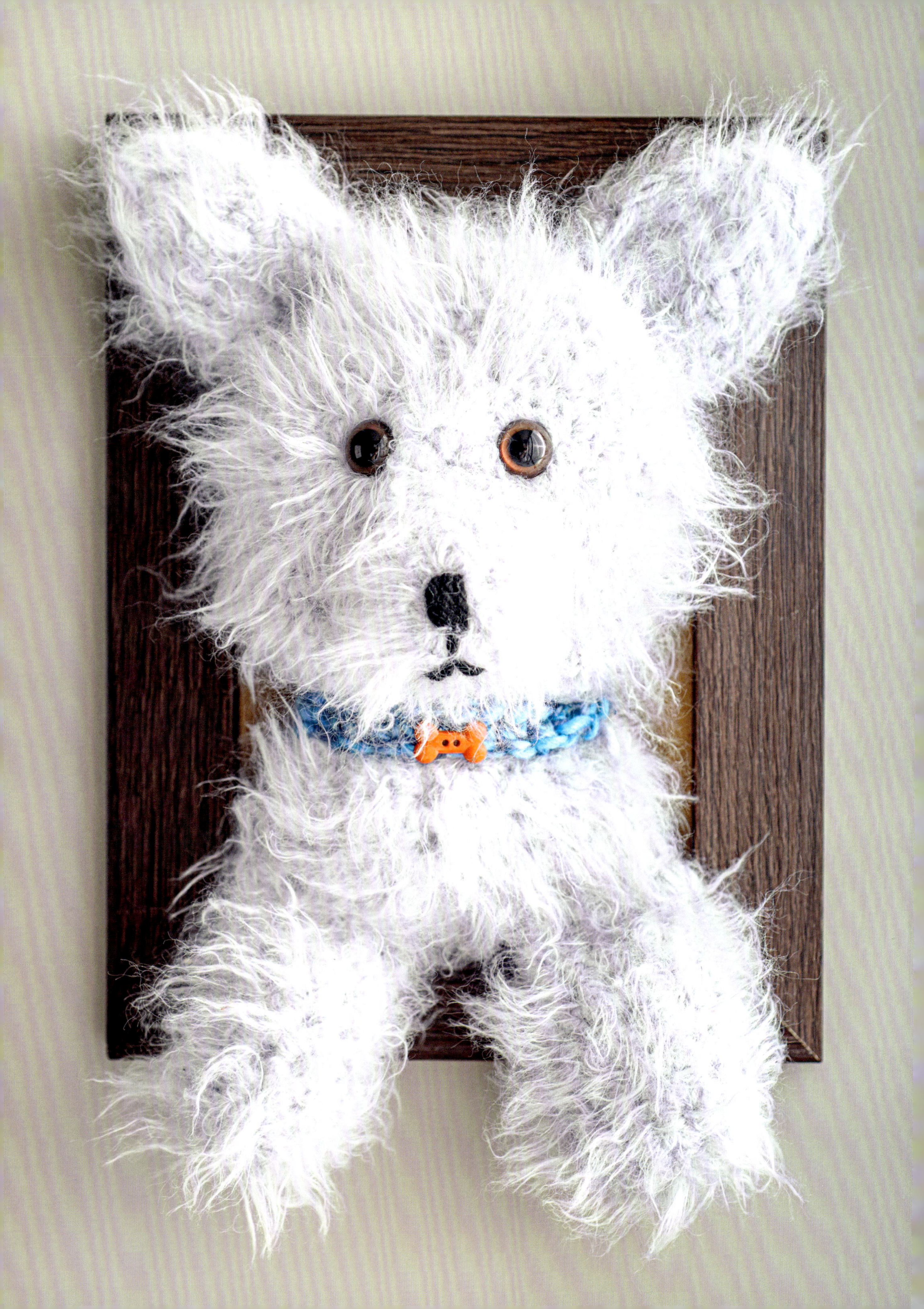

SNOUT
Round 1: Using two strands of A held together, ch4, join with a sl st to form a ring.
Round 2: Ch1 (counts as first sc), 7sc in ring, join with a sl st. (*8 sts*)
Round 3: Ch1, 2sc in next sc, [1sc in next sc, 2sc in next sc] to end, join with a sl st. (*12 sts*)
Rounds 4-7: Ch1, 1sc in next sc, 1sc in each sc to end, join with a sl st.
Fasten off.

EARS
(make 2)
Round 1: Using two strands of A held together, ch4, join with a sl st to form a ring.
Round 2: Ch1 (counts as first sc), 7sc in ring, join with a sl st. (*8 sts*)
Round 3: Ch1, 2sc in next sc, [1sc in next sc, 2sc in next sc] to end, join with a sl st. (*12 sts*)
Round 4: Ch1, 1sc in next sc, 1sc in each sc to end, join with a sl st.
Round 5: Ch1, 1sc in next sc, 2sc in next sc, [1sc in each of next 2 sc, 2sc in next sc] to end, join with a sl st. (*16 sts*)
Rounds 6-10: Ch1, 1sc in next sc, 1sc in each sc to end, join with a sl st.
Fasten off.

PAWS
(make 2)
Round 1: Using two strands of A held together, ch4, join with a sl st to form a ring.
Round 2: Ch1 (counts as first sc), 7sc in ring, join with a sl st. (*8 sts*)
Round 3: Ch1, 2sc in next sc, [1sc in next sc, 2sc in next sc] to end, join with a sl st. (*12 sts*)
Round 4: Ch1, 1sc in next sc, 1sc in each sc to end, join with a sl st.
Round 5: Ch1, 1sc in next sc, 2sc in next sc, [1sc in each of next 2 sc, 2sc in next sc] to end, join with a sl st. (*16 sts*)
Round 6: Ch1, 1sc in next sc, 1sc in each sc to end, join with a sl st.
Round 7: Ch1, 1sc in each of next 2 sc, 2sc in next sc, [1sc in each of next 3 sc, 2sc in next sc] to end, join with a sl st. (*20 sts*)
Rounds 8-11: Ch1, 1sc in next sc, 1sc in each sc to end, join with a sl st.
Fasten off.

COLLAR
Row 1: Using B, ch15. (*15 sts*)
Row 2: 1sc in 2nd ch from hook (missed ch does not count as sc), 1sc in each ch to end. (*14 sts*)
Fasten off.

TO MAKE UP
Stuff the body and sew the seam across to close. Using C, embroider the nose and mouth markings onto the snout using the photo as a guide. Stuff the snout and sew onto the head in the position required. Add the safety eyes above the snout and secure with the backs (see page 141). Stuff the head and sew the open seam closed. Fold each ear in half and sew the open seam closed. Sew the ears on each side of the head. Stuff the paws and sew the open seam closed.

Arrange the head, body, paws, and ears onto the frame, using the photo as a guide for position. Sew the paws onto the body in position required before gluing. Take one piece at a time and glue firmly to the frame backing. Brush gently to give the fluffy fur effect.

Add the collar and glue to the front of the neck. Add any embellishments to the collar.

small framed poodles

Have fun creating these charming little poodle frames to stand on either a table or mantelpiece or to take pride of place on a wall. Easily produced in super bulky yarn, this pattern enables you to make a variety of faces just by changing the shade and length of the fur. It's perfect for using up leftover yarns from your stash.

70 home décor

SKILL RATING ● ○ ○

YARN AND MATERIALS
King Cole Big Value Super Chunky (100% acrylic), super bulky (super chunky) weight yarn, 90yd (81m) per 3½oz (100g) ball
- ½ ball of Champagne 12 (white), Latte 3490 (light brown), or Gray 24 (A)

Small amount of black light worsted (DK) weight yarn (B)

Small amount of toy fiberfill

Pair of ½in (12mm) safety eyes

Fabric glue

7 x 5in (18 x 13cm) photograph frame with glass removed

Bone embellishment (optional)

HOOK AND EQUIPMENT
US H-8 (5mm) crochet hook

Stitch marker

Yarn needle

Stiff brush or pet brush

FINISHED SIZE
7 x 5in (18 x 13cm)

ABBREVIATIONS
See page 142.

POODLE

HEAD
Round 1: Using A, ch4, join with a sl st to form a ring.
Round 2: Ch1 (counts as first sc), 7sc in ring, join with a sl st. (*8 sts*)
Round 3: Ch1, 2sc in next sc, [1sc in next sc, 2sc in next sc] to end, join with a sl st. (*12 sts*)
Round 4: Ch1, 1sc in next sc, 2sc in next sc, [1sc in each of next 2 sc, 2sc in next sc] to end, join with a sl st. (*16 sts*)
Round 5: Ch1, 1sc in each of next 2 sc, 2sc in next sc, [1sc in each of next 3 sc, 2sc in next sc] to end, join with a sl st. (*20 sts*)
Round 6: Ch1, 1sc in each of next 3 sc, 2sc in next sc, [1sc in each of next 4 sc, 2sc in next sc] to end, join with a sl st. (*24 sts*)
(If larger base is required, continue to increase as previous rounds.)
Fasten off.

SNOUT
Round 1: Using A, ch4, join with a sl st to form a ring.
Round 2: Ch1 (counts as first sc), 7sc in ring, join with a sl st. (*8 sts*)
Round 3: Ch1, 2sc in next sc, [1sc in next sc, 2sc in next sc] to end, join with a sl st. (*12 sts*)
Rounds 4 and 5: Ch1, 1sc in next sc, 1sc in each sc to end, join with a sl st.
Fasten off.

TO MAKE UP
Using B, embroider the nose and mouth markings onto the snout. Stuff the snout and sew it to the head. Add the safety eyes above the snout, using the photo as a guide for position, and secure with the backs.

ADDING FUR
Adding the fur on the face can be done in two ways, either with a crochet hook (see page 141) or threading each strand through with a yarn needle and then tying the ends in a knot close to the fabric. The needle is better for getting in small areas, such as around the eyes.

Cut lengths of A approx. 6in (15cm) long. Add a line of fur fringing around the snout and then work outward in lines around the face. Brush with a stiff brush or pet brush to give the fluffy look. Trim to the length or style required.

Fold the brushed fur over the top of the head and glue to hold in place. Add the bone embellishment under the snout (optional).

Glue the head onto the photograph frame.

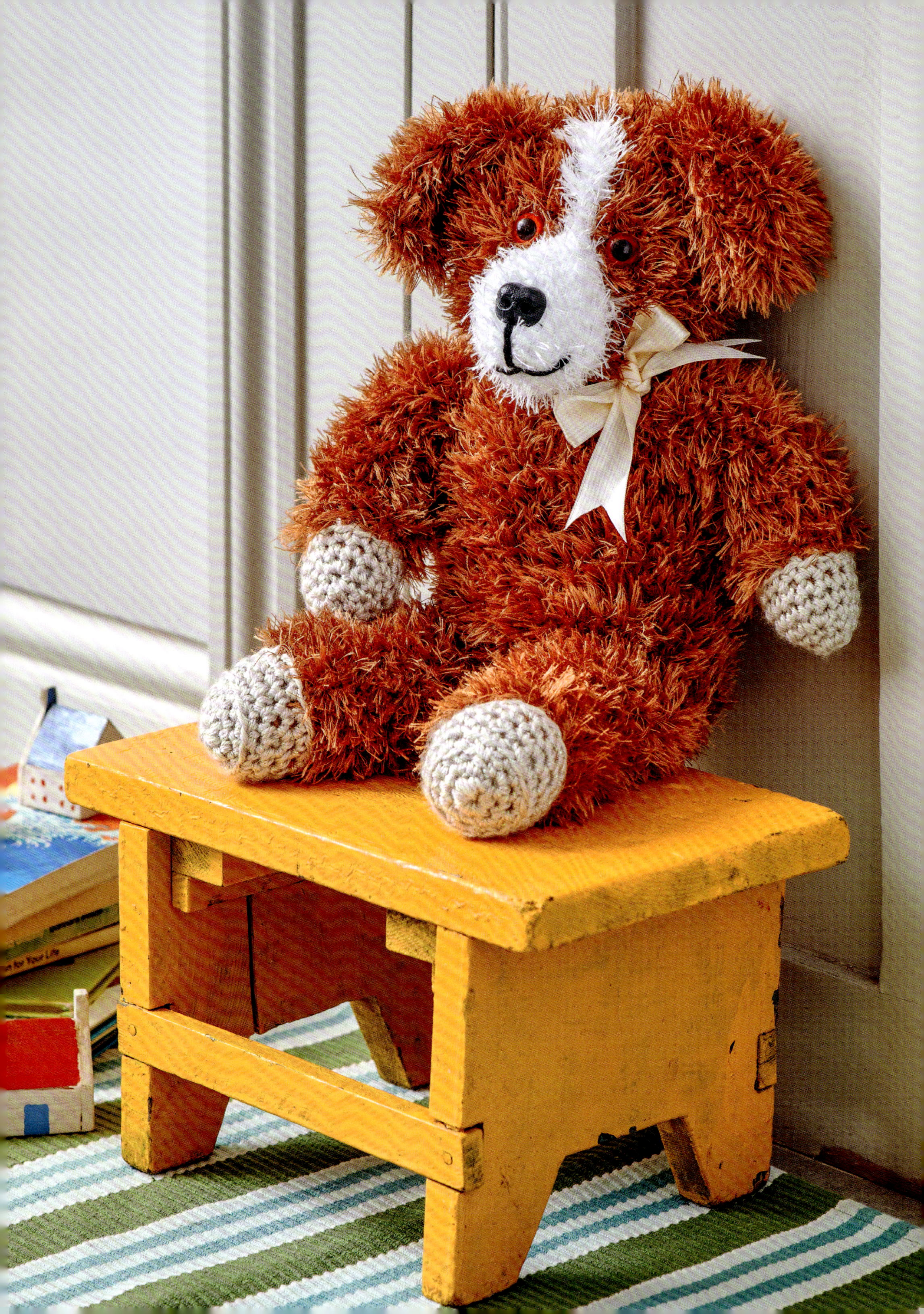

CHAPTER 3

decorative and cuddly dogs

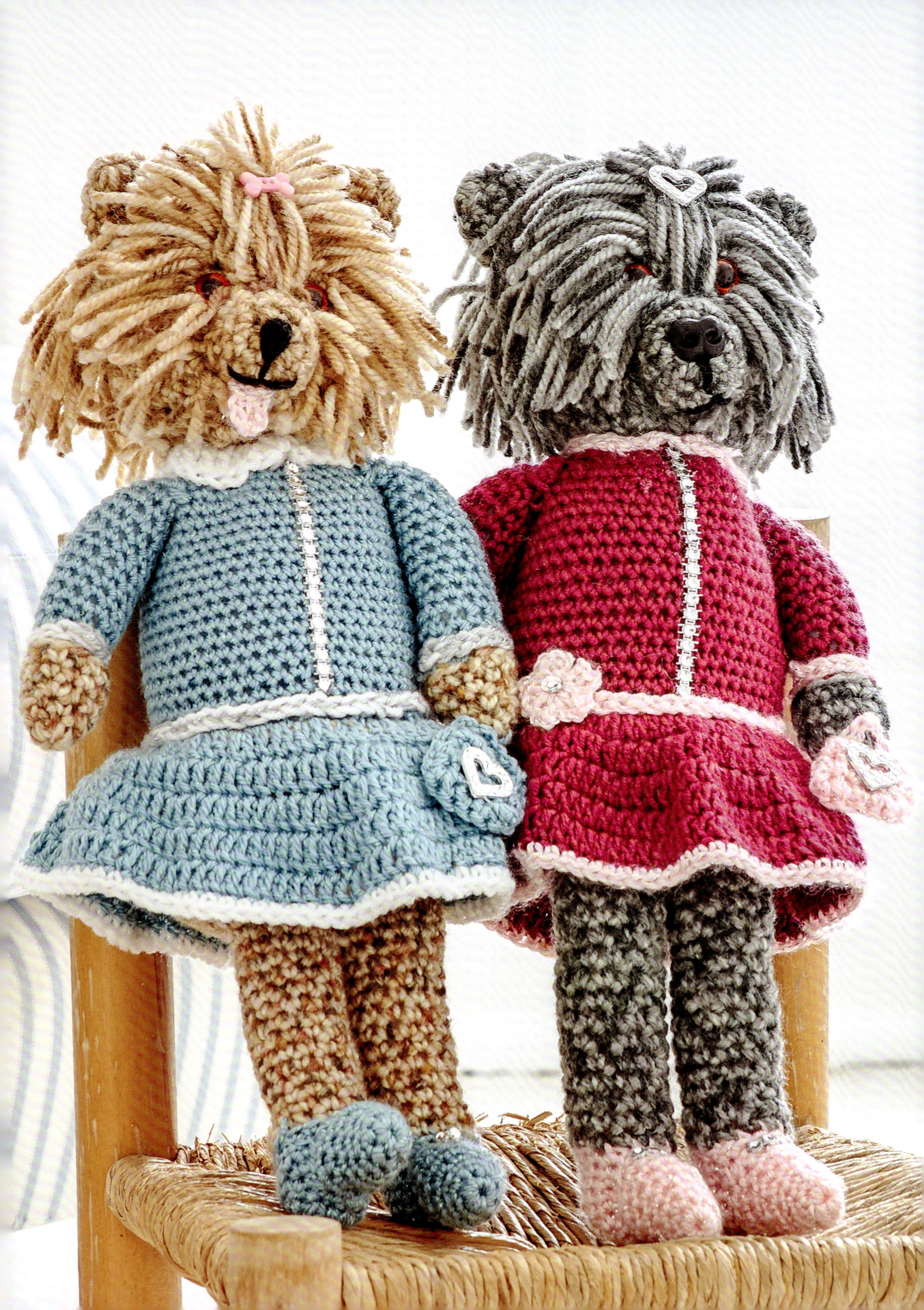

These pretty little terriers would make lovely gifts. They are crocheted in worsted weight yarn, which can be found in any shades to resemble your own faithful pet. Worked mainly in single crochet stitches, with double crochet stitches for the skirt, then the fur is added to the head with strands of yarn and trimmed to the length required. This is a very simple pattern for the beginner.

yorkshire terrier and cairn terrier

SKILL RATING ● ○ ○

YARN AND MATERIALS

Yorkshire terrier
King Cole Bounty Aran (100% acrylic) worsted (Aran) weight yarn, 645yd (587m) per 8¾oz (250g) ball
  ¼ ball of Starling 1752 (brown) (A)

King Cole Glitz DK (97% acrylic, 5% polyester) light worsted (DK) weight yarn, 317yd (290m) per 1¾oz (50g) ball
  1 ball of Sea Breeze 3502 (turquoise blue) (B)
  Small amount of Diamond White 483 (C)
  Small amount of Pink 4721 (D)

Cairn terrier
King Cole Bounty Aran (100% acrylic) worsted (Aran) weight yarn, 645yd (587m) per 8¾oz (250g) ball
  ¼ ball of Marble 1998 (gray) (A)

King Cole Glitz DK (97% acrylic, 5% polyester) light worsted (DK) weight yarn, 317yd (290m) per 1¾oz (50g) ball
  1 ball of Pink Gin 3500 (dark pink) (B)
  Small amount of Pink 4721 (light pink) (C)

Both
Small amount of black light worsted (DK) weight yarn (E)

¾in (20mm) safety nose

Toy fiberfill

Pair of ½in (12mm) safety eyes

Embellishments of your choice

Fabric glue

HOOK AND EQUIPMENT
US G-6 (4mm) crochet hook

Stitch marker

Yarn needle

FINISHED SIZE
Approx. 14in (35.5cm) standing

ABBREVIATIONS
See page 142.

PATTERN NOTES
It is advisable to use a stitch marker with this pattern. If giving the terrier to a young child, substitute the embellishments and the safety nose and eyes with embroidery in yarn (see page 141).

TERRIER
BODY
Worked from bottom upward.
Round 1: Using A, ch4, join with a sl st to form a ring.
Round 2: Ch1 (counts as first sc), 7sc in ring, join with a sl st. (*8 sts*)
Round 3: Ch1, 1sc in same sc, [2sc in next sc] to end, join with a sl st. (*16 sts*)
Round 4: Ch1, 2sc in next sc, [1sc in next sc, 2sc in next sc] to end, join with a sl st. (*24 sts*)
Round 5: Ch1, 1sc in next sc, 2sc in next sc, [1sc in each of next 2 sc, 2sc in next sc] to end, join with a sl st. (*32 sts*)
Round 6: Ch1, 1sc in each of next 2 sc, 2sc in next sc, [1sc in each of next 3 sc, 2sc in next sc] to end, join with a sl st. (*40 sts*)
Round 7: Ch1, 1sc in each of next 3 sc, 2sc in next sc, [1sc in each of next 4 sc, 2sc in next sc] to end, join with a sl st. (*48 sts*)
Round 8: Ch1, 1scBLO in next sc, 1scBLO in each sc to end, join with a sl st.
Rounds 9–15: Ch1, 1sc in next sc, 1sc in each sc to end, join with a sl st.
Fasten off A.
Round 16: Join B, ch1, 1scBLO in next sc, 1scBLO in each sc to end, join with a sl st.
Rounds 17–30: Ch1, 1sc in next sc, 1sc in each sc to end, join with a sl st.
Round 31: Ch1, 1sc in each of next 3 sc, sc2tog, [1sc in each of next 4 sc, sc2tog] to end, join with a sl st. (*40 sts*)
Round 32: Ch1, 1sc in each of next 2 sc, sc2tog, [1sc in each of next 3 sc, sc2tog] to end, join with a sl st. (*32 sts*)
Round 33: Ch1, 1sc in next sc, sc2tog, [1sc in each of next 2 sc, sc2tog] to end, join with a sl st. (*24 sts*)
Round 34: Ch1, sc2tog, [1sc in next sc, sc2tog] to end, join with a sl st. (*16 sts*)
Fasten off.

Skirt
Round 1: On Round 16 of body, join B at center front, ch3 (counts as first dc), 2dcFLO in next sc, [1dcFLO in next sc, 2dcFLO in next sc] to end, join with a sl st. (*72 sts*)
Round 2: Ch3, 1dc in next dc, 1dc in each dc to end, join with a sl st.
Round 3: Ch3, 1dc in next dc, 2dc in next dc, [1dc in each of next 2 dc, 1dc in next dc] to end, join with a sl st. (*96 sts*)
Rounds 4 and 5: Ch3, 1dc in next dc, 1dc in each dc to end, join with a sl st.
Fasten off B.
Round 6: Join C, ch1 (counts as first sc), 1sc in next dc, 1sc in each dc to end, join with a sl st.
Fasten off.

COLLAR
Row 1: Using C, ch33.
Row 2: 1sc in 2nd ch from hook (missed ch does not count as sc), 1sc in each sc to end. (*32 sts*)
Fasten off.

HEAD
Round 1: Using A, ch4, join with a sl st to form a ring.
Round 2: Ch1 (counts as first sc), 7sc in ring, join with a sl st. (*8 sts*)
Round 3: Ch1, 1sc in same sc, [2sc in next sc] to end, join with a sl st. (*16 sts*)
Round 4: Ch1, 2sc in next sc, [1sc in next sc, 2sc in next sc] to end, join with a sl st. (*24 sts*)
Round 5: Ch1, 1sc in next sc, 1sc in each sc to end, join with a sl st.
Round 6: Ch1, 1sc in next sc, 2sc in next sc, [1sc in each of next 2 sc, 2sc in next sc] to end, join with a sl st. (*32 sts*)
Round 7: Ch1, 1sc in next sc, 1sc in each sc to end, join with a sl st.
Round 8: Ch1, 1sc in each of next 2 sc, 2sc in next sc, [1sc in each of next 3 sc, 2sc in next sc] to end, join with a sl st. (*40 sts*)
Rounds 9–16: Ch1, 1sc in next sc, 1sc in each sc to end, join with a sl st.
Round 17: Ch1, 1sc in next sc, sc2tog, [1sc in each of next 2 sc, sc2tog] to end, join with a sl st. (*30 sts*)
Round 18: Ch1, sc2tog, [1sc in next sc, sc2tog] to end, join with a sl st. (*20 sts*)
Rounds 19 and 20: Ch1, 1sc in next sc, 1sc in each sc to end, join with a sl st.
Fasten off.

EARS
(make 2)
Round 1: Using A, ch4, join with a sl st to form a ring.
Round 2: Ch1 (counts as first sc), 7sc in ring, join with a sl st. (*8 sts*)
Round 3: Ch1, 2sc in next sc, [1sc in next sc, 2sc in next sc] to end, join with a sl st. (*12 sts*)
Rounds 4–6: Ch1, 1sc in next sc, 1sc in each sc to end, join with a sl st.
Fasten off.
Fold in half and join the seam.

SNOUT
Round 1: Using A, ch4, join with a sl st to form a ring.
Round 2: Ch1 (counts as first sc), 7sc in ring, join with a sl st. (*8 sts*)
Round 3: Ch1, 2sc in next sc, [1sc in next sc, 2sc in next sc] to end, join with a sl st. (*12 sts*)
Rounds 4–6: Ch1, 1sc in next sc, 1sc in each sc to end, join with a sl st.
Fasten off.

TONGUE
(Optional)
Row 1: Using D, ch4, 1sc in 2nd ch from hook (missed ch does not count as sc), 1sc in each ch to end. (*3 sts*)
Row 2: Ch1 (counts as first sc), 1sc in next sc, 1sc in each sc to end.
Fasten off.

ARMS
(make 2)
Round 1: Using A, ch4, join with a sl st to form a ring.
Round 2: Ch1 (counts as first sc), 7sc in ring, join with a sl st to first sc. (*8 sts*)
Round 3: Ch1, 1sc in next sc, 1sc in each sc to end, join with a sl st.
Round 4: Ch1, 2sc in next sc, [1sc in next sc, 2sc in next sc] to end, join with a sl st. (*12 sts*)
Rounds 5 and 6: Ch1, 1sc in next sc, 1sc in each sc to end, join with a sl st.
Fasten off A.
Round 7: Join B, ch1, 1scBLO next sc, 1scBLO in each sc to end, join with a sl st.
Rounds 8-22: Ch1, 1sc in next sc, 1sc in each sc to end, join with a sl st.
Fasten off.

LEGS
(make 2)
Round 1: Using B for Yorkshire or C for Cairn, ch5, join with a sl st to form a ring.
Round 2: Ch1 (counts as first sc), 9sc in ring, join with a sl st. (*10 sts*)
Round 3: Ch1, 2sc in next sc, [1sc in next sc, 2sc in next sc] to end, join with a sl st. (*15 sts*)
Rounds 4-8: Ch1, 1sc in next sc, 1sc in each sc to end, join with a sl st.
Fasten off B or C.
Round 9: Join A, ch1, 1scBLO in next sc, 1scBLO in each sc to end, join with a sl st.
Round 10: Ch1, 1sc in each of next 2 sc, sc2tog, [1sc in each of next 3sc, sc2tog] to end, join with a sl st. (*12 sts*)
Rounds 11-26: Ch1, 1sc in next sc, 1sc in each sc to end, join with a sl st.
Fasten off.

SHOE FOOT
Round 1: Using B for Yorkshire or C for Cairn, ch4, join with a sl st to form a ring.
Round 2: Ch1 (counts as first sc), 7sc in ring, join with a sl st. (*8 sts*)
Rounds 3 and 4: Ch1, 1sc in next sc, 1sc in each sc to end, join with a sl st.
Round 5: Ch1, 2sc in next sc, [1sc in next sc, 2sc in next sc] to end, join with a sl st. (*12 sts*)
Rounds 6-8: Ch1, 1sc in next sc, 1sc in each sc to end, join with a sl st.
Fasten off.

HANDBAG
Row 1: Using B for Yorkshire or C for Cairn, ch6.
Row 2: 1sc in 2nd ch from hook (missed ch does not count as sc), 1sc in each ch to end. (*5 sts*)
Rows 3-10: Ch1, 1sc in next sc, 1sc in each sc to end. Ch8, for handle.
Fasten off.
Fold bag in half and sew seam on both sides leaving the top edge open. Sew end of ch to other side at top of the bag to form handle.

FLOWER
(optional)
Row 1: Using C, ch4, join with a sl st to form a ring.
Row 2: [Sl st, ch2, 1dc, ch2] five times into ring, sl st into ring. (*5 petals*)
Fasten off.

yorkshire terrier and cairn terrier

TO MAKE UP

Using E, embroider the mouth markings to the snout (see page 141) in positions required, using the photo as a guide. Add the nose and secure with the safety back (see page 141). Stuff the snout and sew to the front of the head.

Attach the eyes to the head and secure the backs. Stuff the head then sew on the ears using the photo as a guide.

Stuff the body and then sew on the head. Stuff the arms and sew the seam across the top. Sew the arms to the body.

Stuff the legs. If your terrier is to be sitting, fold the top of leg in half and join the seam. If your terrier is to be standing, leave the leg gap open. Sew the legs to the body in the positions required.

Stuff the shoe foot and sew to front of each leg. Sew the collar to the dress.

For the edging around the waist and edge of cuffs, crochet lengths of chain in C to fit, and sew in place. Sew the flower to the waist if desired.

ADDING FUR

Adding the fur on the face can be done in two ways, either with a crochet hook (see page 141) or threading each strand through with a yarn needle and then tying the ends into a knot close to the fabric. The needle is better for getting into small areas, such as around the eyes.

Ponytail

Cut lengths of A to 6in (15cm). Start by working several lines of fur fringing above the snout for the little ponytail. Tie with a length of yarn and then use A to sew to the head to secure.

Head

Continue to add fur fringing around and under the snout. Trim any excess fur to produce the length required. Continue all around the face and around the ears. For the back of the head use longer lengths of yarn; to give volume it is advisable to work two rows approx. 2in (5cm) apart to cover the back of the head. Trim to the length required.

Sew the handbag to the end of the hand.

Decorate your terrier with your chosen embellishments.

chihuahua nutcracker

This charming Chihuahua nutcracker will be the center of attention and brighten up any festive display, and it also makes a great gift for the holiday season. If you're giving it to a young child, the nose and eyes can easily be embroidered in black yarn instead. Crocheted in single crochet and festive light worsted yarn with its unique sparkle, this will be a real head-turner at Christmas.

SKILL RATING ● ● ●

YARN AND MATERIALS
King Cole Glitz DK (97% acrylic, 5% polyester) light worsted (DK) weight yarn, 317yd (290m) per 3½oz (100g) ball
- 1 ball of Christmas 1698 (red, white, and green) (A)
- 1 ball of Diamond White 483 (D)
- Small amount of Christmas Green 3307 (E)

King Cole Moments DK (100% polyester) light worsted (DK) weight yarn, 98yd (90m) per 1¾oz (50g) ball
- 1 ball of Koala 499 (dark brown) (B)
- Small amount of White 470 (C)

Small amount of black light worsted (DK) weight yarn (F)

Toy fiberfill

¾in (20mm) safety nose

Pair of ⅝in (15mm) safety eyes

Embellishments of your choice

HOOK AND EQUIPMENT
US G-6 (4mm) crochet hook

Stitch marker

Yarn needle

FINISHED SIZE
Approx. 18in (45.5cm) standing

ABBREVIATIONS
See page 142.

PATTERN NOTES
It is advisable to use a stitch marker with this pattern.
If giving the nutcracker to a young child, substitute the embellishments and the safety nose and eyes with embroidery in yarn (see page 141).

CHIHAUHUA
BODY
Worked from bottom upward.
Round 1: Using A, ch4, join with a sl st to form a ring.
Round 2: Ch1 (counts as first sc), 7sc in ring, join with a sl st. (*8 sts*)
Round 3: Ch1, 1sc in same sc, [2sc in next sc] to end, join with a sl st. (*16 sts*)
Round 4: Ch1, 2sc in next sc, [1sc in next sc, 2sc in next sc] to end, join with a sl st. (*24 sts*)
Round 5: Ch1, 1sc in next sc, 2sc in next sc, [1sc in each of next 2 sc, 2sc in next sc] to end, join with a sl st. (*32 sts*)
Round 6: Ch1, 1sc in each of next 2 sc, 2sc in next sc, [1sc in each of next 3 sc, 2sc in next sc] to end, join with a sl st. (*40 sts*)
Round 7: Ch1, 1sc in each of next 3 sc, 2sc in next sc, [1sc in each of next 4 sc, 2sc in next sc] to end, join with a sl st. (*48 sts*)
Round 8: Ch1, 1sc in each of next 4 sc, 2sc in next sc, [1sc in each of next 5 sc, 2sc in next sc] to end, join with a sl st. (*56 sts*)
Round 9: Ch1, 1scBLO in next sc, 1scBLO in each sc to end, join with a sl st.
Rounds 10 and 11: Ch1, 1sc in next sc, 1sc in each sc to end, join with a sl st.
Round 12: Ch1, 1scBLO in next sc, 1scBLO in each sc to end, join with a sl st.
Rounds 13-34: Ch1, 1sc in next sc, 1sc in each sc to end, join with a sl st.
Round 35: Ch1, 1sc in each of next 4 sc, sc2tog, [1sc in each of next 5 sc, sc2tog] to end, join with a sl st. (*48 sts*)
Round 36: Ch1, 1sc in each of next 3 sc, sc2tog, [1sc in each of next 4 sc, sc2tog] to end, join with a sl st. (*40 sts*)
Round 37: Ch1, 1sc in each of next 2 sc, sc2tog, [1sc in each of next 3 sc, sc2tog] to end, join with a sl st. (*32 sts*)
Round 38: Ch1, 1sc in next sc, sc2tog, [1sc in each of next 2 sc, sc2tog] to end, join with a sl st. (*24 sts*)
Round 39: Ch1, sc2tog, [1sc in next sc, sc2tog] to end, join with a sl st. (*16 sts*)
Fasten off.

80 decorative and cuddly dogs

Bottom of jacket
Round 1: On Round 12 of body, join A at center front, ch3 (counts as first dc), 1dcFLO in same sc, [1dcFLO in next sc, 2dcFLO in next sc] to last st, turn work leaving last st unworked, do not join. (*83 sts*)
Rounds 2 and 3: Ch3, 1dc in next dc, 1dc in each dc to end, join with a sl st.
Fasten off.

HEAD
Round 1: Using B, ch4, join with a sl st to form a ring.
Round 2: Ch1 (counts as first sc), 7sc in ring, join with a sl st. (*8 sts*)
Round 3: Ch1, 1sc in same sc, [2sc in next sc] to end, join with a sl st. (*16 sts*)
Round 4: Ch1, 2sc in next sc, [1sc in next sc, 2sc in next sc] to end, join with a sl st. (*24 sts*)
Round 5: Ch1, 1sc in next sc, 2sc in next sc, [1sc in each of next 2 sc, 2sc in next sc] to end, join with a sl st. (*32 sts*)
Round 6: Ch1, 1sc in each of next 2 sc, 2sc in next sc, [1sc in each of next 3 sc, 2sc in next sc] to end, join with a sl st. (*40 sts*)
Round 7: Ch1, 1sc in next sc, 1sc in each sc to end, join with a sl st.
Round 8: Ch1, 1sc in each of next 3 sc, 2sc in next sc, [1sc in each of next 4 sc, 2sc in next sc] to end, join with a sl st. (*48 sts*)
Rounds 9–20: Ch1, 1sc in next sc, 1sc in each sc to end, join with a sl st.
Round 21: Ch1, 1sc in each of next 3 sc, sc2tog, [1sc in each of next 4 sc, sc2tog] to end, join with a sl st. (*40 sts*)
Round 22: Ch1, 1sc in each of next 2 sc, sc2tog, [1sc in each of next 3 sc, sc2tog] to end, join with a sl st. (*32 sts*)
Round 23: Ch1, 1sc in next sc, 1sc in each sc to end, join with a sl st.
Round 24: Ch1, 1sc in next sc, sc2tog, [1sc in each of next 2 sc, sc2tog] to end, join with a sl st. (*24 sts*)
Round 25: Ch1, sc2tog, [1sc in next sc, sc2tog] to end, join with a sl st. (*16 sts*)
Fasten off.

STRIPE ABOVE SNOUT
Row 1: Using C, ch11.
Row 2: 1sc in 2nd ch from hook (missed ch does not count as sc), 1sc in each ch to end. (*10 sts*)
Row 3: Ch1 (counts as first sc), 1sc in next sc, 1sc in each sc to end.
Fasten off.

SNOUT
Round 1: Using C, ch4, join with a sl st to form a ring.
Round 2: Ch1 (counts as first sc), 7sc in ring, join with a sl st to first sc. (*8 sts*)
Round 3: Ch1, 1sc in same sc, [2sc in next sc] to end, join with a sl st. (*16 sts*)
Rounds 4–6: Ch1, 1sc in next sc, 1sc in each sc to end, join with a sl st.
Fasten off.

chihuahua nutcracker

EARS

(make 2)

Row 1: Using B, ch2.
Row 2: 1sc in 2nd ch from hook (missed ch does not count as sc). (*1 st*)
Row 3: Ch1 (counts as first sc), 1sc in same sc. (*2 sts*)
Row 4: Ch1, 1sc in same sc, 1sc in each sc to end. (*3 sts*)
Row 5: Ch1, 1sc in same sc, 1sc in each sc to end. (*4 sts*)
Row 6: Ch1, 1sc in same sc, 1sc in each sc to end. (*5 sts*)
Row 7: Ch1, 1sc in same sc, 1sc in each sc to end. (*6 sts*)
Row 8: Ch1, 1sc in same sc, 1sc in each sc to end. (*7 sts*)
Row 9: Ch1, 1sc in same sc, 1sc in each sc to end. (*8 sts*)
Fasten off.

ARMS

(make 2)

Round 1: Using D, ch4, join with a sl st to form a ring.
Round 2: Ch1 (counts as first sc), 7sc in ring, join with a sl st. (*8 sts*)
Round 3: Ch1, 1sc in same sc, [2sc in next sc] to end, join with a sl st. (*16 sts*)
Rounds 4 and 5: Ch1, 1sc in next sc, 1sc in each sc to end, join with a sl st.
Fasten off D.
Round 6: Join A, ch1, 1scBLO in next sc, 1scBLO in each sc to end, join with a sl st.
Rounds 7–22: Ch1, 1sc in next sc, 1sc in each sc to end, join with a sl st.
Stuff firmly.
Round 23: Join B, ch1, 1scBLO in next sc, 1scBLO in each sc to end, join with a sl st.
Rounds 24 and 25: Ch1, 1sc in next sc, 1sc in each sc to end, join with a sl st.
Round 26: Ch1, 1sc in next sc, sc2tog, [1sc in each of next 2 sc, sc2tog] to end, join with a sl st. (*12 sts*)
Cont to stuff firmly.
Round 27: Ch1, sc2tog, [1sc in next sc, sc2tog] to end, join with a sl st. (*8 sts*)
Fasten off, leaving a length of yarn.
Thread end onto needle, gather remaining sts together. Fasten off.

BOOT TOPS AND LEGS

(make 2)

Round 1: Using E, ch4, join with a sl st to form a ring.
Round 2: Ch1 (counts as first sc), 7sc in ring, join with a sl st. (*8 sts*)
Round 3: Ch1, 2sc in next sc, [1sc in next sc, 2sc in next sc] to end, join with a sl st. (*12 sts*)
Round 4: Ch1, 2sc in next sc, [1sc in next sc, 2sc in next sc] to end, join with a sl st. (*18 sts*)
Round 5: Ch1, 1scBLO in next sc, 1scBLO in each sc to end, join with a sl st.
Rounds 6–14: Ch1, 1sc in next sc, 1sc in each sc to end, join with a sl st.
Fasten off E. Stuff firmly.
Round 15: Join D, ch1, 1scBLO in next sc, 1scBLO in each sc to end, join with a sl st.
Rounds 16–35: Ch1, 1sc in next sc, 1sc in each sc to end, join with a sl st.
Fasten off.

BOOT FOOT
(make 2)

Round 1: Using E, ch4, join with a sl st to form a ring.
Round 2: Ch1 (counts as first sc), 7sc in ring, join with a sl st in first sc. (*8 sts*)
Round 3: Ch1, 2sc in next sc, [1sc in next sc, 2sc in next sc] to end, join with a sl st. (*12 sts*)
Round 4: Ch1, 1sc in next sc, 1sc in each sc to end, join with a sl st.
Round 5: Ch1, 1sc in next sc, 2sc in next sc, [1sc in each of next 2 sc, 2sc in next sc] to end, join with a sl st. (*16 sts*)
Rounds 6-8: Ch1, 1sc in next sc, 1sc in each sc to end, join with a sl st.
Round 9: Ch1, 1sc in each of next 2 sc, 2sc in next sc, [1sc in each of next 3 sc, 2sc in next sc] to end, join with a sl st. (*20 sts*)
Fasten off.

HAT

Round 1: Using D, ch4, join with a sl st to form a ring.
Round 2: Ch1 (counts as first sc), 9sc in ring, join with a sl st. (*10 sts*)
Round 3: Ch1, 1sc in same sc, [2sc in next sc] to end, join with a sl st. (*20 sts*)
Round 4: Ch1, 2sc in next sc, [1sc in next sc, 2sc in next sc] to end, join with a sl st. (*30 sts*)
Round 5: Ch1, 1sc in next sc, 2sc in next sc, [1sc in each of next 2 sc, 2sc in next sc] to end, join with a sl st. (*40 sts*)
Round 6: Ch1, 1scBLO in next sc, 1scBLO in each sc to end, join with a sl st.
Rounds 7-12: Ch1, 1sc in next sc, 1sc in each sc to end, join with a sl st.
Fasten off D.
Round 13: Join A, ch1, 1sc in next sc, 1sc in each sc to end, join with a sl st.
Round 14: Ch1, 1sc in next sc, sc2tog, [1sc in each of next 2 sc, sc2tog] to end, join with a sl st. (*30 sts*)
Round 15: Ch1, sc2tog, [1sc in next sc, sc2tog] to end, join with a sl st. (*20 sts*)
Fasten off.

TO MAKE UP

Using F, embroider the mouth markings on the snout (see page 141) using the photo as a guide. Add the nose to the snout and secure with the safety back (see page 141). Stuff the snout firmly. Sew the snout to the head in the position required. Add the eyes to the head in the positions required and secure with safety backs. Stuff the head firmly. Sew the ears to the head in the positions required.

Stuff the body firmly then sew the head to the body. Sew the arms to the body with the top of each of the arms in line with the shoulders.

Stuff the legs firmly. If your nutcracker is to be sitting, fold the top of the leg in half and join the seam. If your nutcracker is to be standing, leave the leg gap open. Sew the legs to the body in the positions required.

Stuff the front foot of the boots and sew to the front of the legs at the bottom to form the boots.

Holding two strands of A held together, work slip stitch surface crochet (see page 140) along Round 6 of the hat. Tie yarn ends and trim, leaving the ends loose to form tassels. Stuff the hat and sew to the head.

Decorate your nutcracker with your chosen embellishments.

chihuahua nutcracker

What a great companion for a child to cuddle! Crocheted in single crochet stitch throughout with a very soft yarn, this would also make a lovely gift for adults.

spaniel cuddle buddy

SPANIEL

HEAD
Row 1: Using two strands of A held together, ch33.
Row 2: 1sc in 2nd ch from hook (missed ch does not count as sc), 1sc in each ch to end. (*32 sts*)
Rows 3-14: Ch1 (counts as first sc), 1sc in next sc, 1sc in each sc to end.
Fasten off.

TOP OF HEAD
Round 1: Using two strands of A held together, ch4, join with a sl st to form a ring.
Round 2: Ch1 (counts as first sc), 7sc in ring, join with a sl st. (*8 sts*)
Round 3: Ch1, 1sc in same sc, [2sc in next sc] to end, join with a sl st. (*16 sts*)
Round 4: Ch1, 2sc in next sc, [1sc in next sc, 2sc in next sc] to end, join with a sl st. (*24 sts*)
Round 5: Ch1, 1sc in next sc, 2sc in next sc, [1sc in each of next 2 sc, 2sc in next sc] to end, join with a sl st. (*32 sts*)
Fasten off.

BODY
Round 1: Using two strands of A held together, ch4, join with a sl st to form a ring.
Round 2: Ch1 (counts as first sc), 7sc in ring, join with a sl st. (*8 sts*)
Round 3: Ch1, 1sc in same sc, [2sc in next sc] to end, join with a sl st. (*16 sts*)
Round 4: Ch1, 2sc in next sc, [1sc in next sc, 2sc in next sc] to end, join with a sl st. (*24 sts*)
Round 5: Ch1, 1sc in same sc, [2sc in next sc] twice, 1sc in each of next 9 sc, [2sc in next sc] three times, 1sc in next 9 sc, join with a sl st. (*30 sts*)
Round 6: Ch1, 1sc in same sc, [2sc in next sc] twice, 1sc in each of next 12 sc, [2sc in next sc] three times, 1sc in next 12 sc, join with a sl st. (*36 sts*)
Round 7: Ch1, 1sc in same sc, 2sc in next sc, 1sc in each of next 16 sc, [2sc in next sc] twice, 1sc in next 16 sc, join with a sl st. (*40 sts*)
Round 8: Ch1, 1scBLO in next sc, 1scBLO in each sc to end, join with a sl st.
Round 9: Ch1, 1sc in next sc, 1sc in each sc to end, join with a sl st.
Round 10: Ch1, 1sc in each of next 3 sc, 2sc in next sc, [1sc in each of next 4 sc, 2sc in next sc] to end, join with a sl st. (*48 sts*)

SKILL RATING ● ● ●

YARN AND MATERIALS
King Cole Moments DK (100% polyester) light worsted (DK) weight yarn, 98yd (90m) per 1¾oz (50g) ball
  6 balls of Ginger 1876 (orange brown) (A)
  1 ball of White 470 (B)

King Cole Glitz DK (97% acrylic, 3% polyester) light worsted (DK) weight yarn, 317yd (290m) per 3½oz (100g) ball
  ½ ball of Silver 565 (gray) (C)

Small amount of black light worsted (DK) weight yarn (D)

⅞in (22mm) safety nose

Toy fiberfill

Pair of ⅝in (15mm) safety eyes

Short length of ribbon (optional)

HOOK AND EQUIPMENT
US H-8 (5mm) crochet hook
Stitch marker
Yarn needle
Pins

FINISHED SIZE
Approx. 18in (46cm) tall

ABBREVIATIONS
See page 142.

PATTERN NOTES
All yarns are worked with two strands of yarn held together.
If giving the spaniel to a young child, substitute the safety nose and eyes with embroidery in black yarn (see page 141).

decorative and cuddly dogs

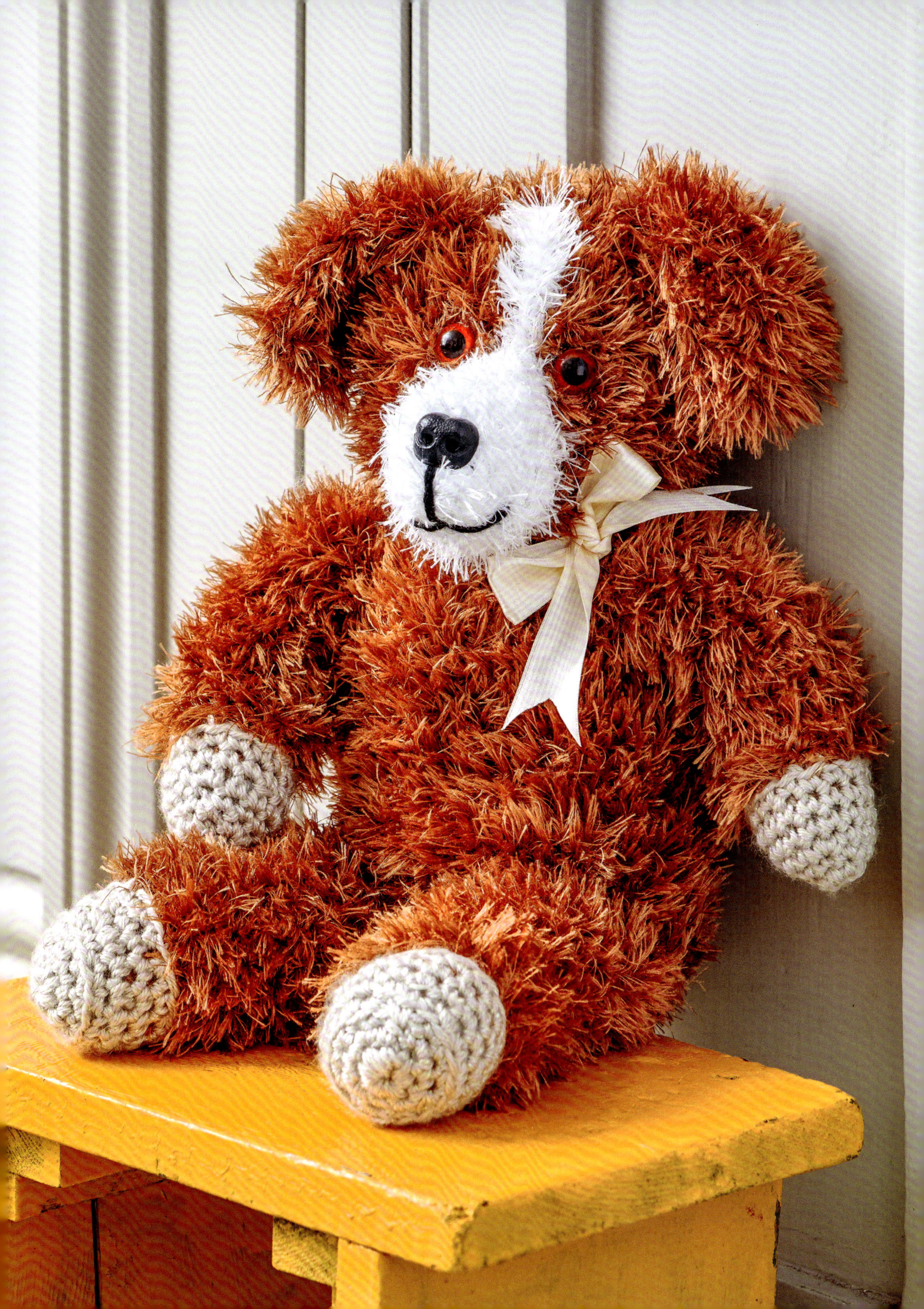

Rounds 11–24: Ch1, 1sc in next sc, 1sc in each sc to end, join with a sl st.
Round 25: Ch1, 1sc in each of next 3 sc, sc2tog, [1sc in each of next 4 sc, sc2tog] to end, join with a sl st. (*40 sts*)
Round 26: Ch1, 1sc in next sc, sc2tog, [1sc in each of next 2 sc, sc2tog] to end, join with a sl st. (*30 sts*)
Round 27: Ch1, sc2tog, [1sc in next sc, sc2tog] to end, join with a sl st. (*20 sts*)
Round 28: Ch1, 1sc in next sc, 1sc in each sc to end, join with a sl st.
Stuff body firmly.
Round 29: [Sc2tog] to end, join with a sl st. (*10 sts*)
Fasten off, leaving a length of yarn. Thread end onto needle and gather remaining sts together.

SNOUT
Round 1: Using two strands of B held together, ch4, join with a sl st to form a ring.
Round 2: Ch1 (counts as first sc), 7sc in ring, join with a sl st. (*8 sts*)
Round 3: Ch1, 1sc in next sc, 1sc in each sc to end, join with a sl st.
Round 4: Ch1, 2sc in next sc, [1sc in next sc, 2sc in next sc] to end, join with a sl st. (*12 sts*)
Round 5: Ch1, 1sc in next sc, 1sc in each sc to end, join with a sl st.
Round 6: Ch1, 1sc in next sc, 2sc in next sc, [1sc in each of next 2 sc, 2sc in next sc] to end, join with a sl st. (*16 sts*)
Rounds 7 and 8: Ch1, 1sc in next sc, 1sc in each sc to end, join with a sl st.
Round 9: Ch1, 1sc in each of next 2 sc, 2sc in next sc, [1sc in each of next 3 sc, 2sc in next sc] to end, join with a sl st. (*20 sts*)
Rounds 10 and 11: Ch1, 1sc in next sc, 1sc in each sc to end, join with a sl st.
Do not fasten off.

Forehead stripe
Row 1: Ch11, 1sc in 2nd ch from hook (missed ch does not count as sc), 1sc in each ch to end. (*10 sts*)
Row 2: Ch1 (counts as first sc), 1sc in next sc, 1sc in each sc to end.
Fasten off.

EARS
(make 2)
Row 1: Using two strands of A held together, ch8.
Row 2: 1sc in 2nd ch from hook (missed ch does not count as sc), 1sc in each ch to end. (*7 sts*)
Rows 3–14: Ch1 (counts as first sc), 1sc in next sc, 1sc in each sc to end.
Fasten off.

ARMS
(make 2)

Round 1: Using two strands of C held together, ch4, join with a sl st to form a ring.
Round 2: Ch1 (counts as first sc), 7sc in ring, join with a sl st. (*8 sts*)
Round 3: Ch1, 2sc in next sc, [1sc in next sc, 2sc in next sc] to end, join with a sl st. (*12 sts*)
Round 4: Ch1, 1sc in next sc, 1sc in each sc to end, join with a sl st.
Round 5: Ch1, 1sc in next sc, 2sc in next sc, [1sc in each of next 2 sc, 2sc in next sc] to end, join with a sl st. (*16 sts*)
Rounds 6 and 7: Ch1, 1sc in next sc, 1sc in each sc to end, join with a sl st.
Fasten off C, join in two strands of A held together.
Round 8: Ch1, 1scBLO in next sc, 1scBLO in each sc to end, join with a sl st.
Rounds 9-22: Ch1, 1sc in next sc, 1sc in each sc to end, join with a sl st.
Fasten off.

LEGS
(make 2)

Round 1: Using two strands of C held together, ch4, join with a sl st to form a ring.
Round 2: Ch1 (counts as first sc), 7sc in ring, join with a sl st. (*8 sts*)
Round 3: Ch1, 2sc in next sc, [1sc in next sc, 2sc in next sc] to end, join with a sl st. (*12 sts*)
Round 4: Ch1, 1sc in next sc, 2sc in next sc, [1sc in each of next 2 sc, 2sc in next sc] to end, join with a sl st. (*16 sts*)
Round 5: Ch1, 1scBLO in next sc, 1scBLO in each sc to end, join with a sl st.
Rounds 6-8: Ch1, 1sc in next sc, 1sc in each sc to end, join with a sl st.
Fasten off C, join in two strands of A held together.
Round 9: Ch1, 1scBLO in next sc, 1scBLO in each sc to end, join with a sl st.
Rounds 10-24: Ch1, 1sc in next sc, 1sc in each sc to end, join with a sl st.
Fasten off.

TO MAKE UP
Working on the wrong side, sew the seam on the head together. Pin the top of the head onto the head and then sew in place. Turn to right side.

Using D, sew the stitches for the mouth on the snout (see page 141). Insert the safety nose using the photo as a guide for position and secure with the back (see page 141). Stuff the snout and then sew to the head, also sewing the stripe in place.

Add the safety eyes and secure with the backs. Stuff the head firmly and then gather the stitches together at the bottom of the head to close the opening. Sew the head to the body. Sew the ears to the head using the photo as a guide for position.

Stuff the arms and the legs and sew the end of each closed. Sew the arms and legs to the body, using the photo as a guide for position.

Tie the ribbon in a bow around the neck for decoration (optional).

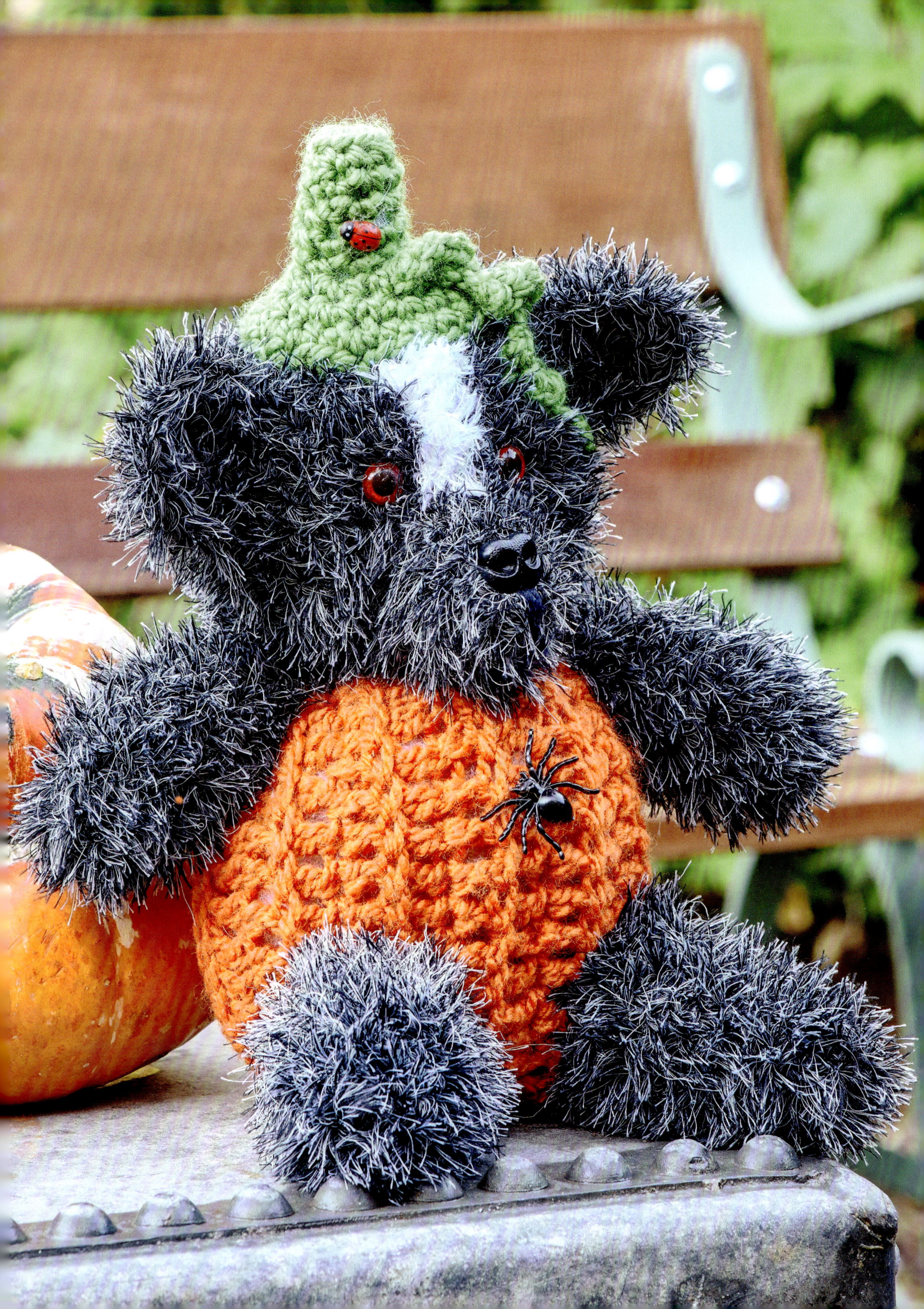

This bright little fellow with his cheeky furry face will make a perfect decoration for any Halloween table or doorstop, and will charm all ages. He is worked in a mixture of single crochet, half double crochet, and double crochet stitches throughout.

pomeranian pumpkin pal

SKILL RATING ●●○

YARN AND MATERIALS
King Cole Big Value Chunky (100% acrylic), bulky (chunky) weight yarn, 167yd (152m) per 3½oz (100g) ball
 ½ ball of Mango 1746 (orange) (A)
 Small amount of Green 833 (D)

King Cole Moments DK (100% polyester) light worsted (DK) weight yarn, 98yd (90m) per 1¾oz (50g) ball
 5 balls of Badger 498 (dark gray) (B)
 Small amount of White 470 (C)

Small amount of black or dark blue light worsted (DK) weight yarn (E)

Toy fiberfill

¾in (20mm) safety nose

Pair of ½in (14mm) safety eyes

Spider and ladybug embellishments

HOOK AND EQUIPMENT
US H-8 (5mm) crochet hook
Stitch marker
Yarn needle

FINISHED SIZE
Approx. 10in (25.5cm) tall when sitting

ABBREVIATIONS
See page 142.

PATTERN NOTES
Moments DK (yarns B and C) is worked with two strands of yarn held together throughout; it is advisable to use a stitch marker when working with this yarn.
If giving the Pomeranian to a young child, substitute the embellishments and the safety nose and eyes with embroidery in yarn (see page 141).

BODY
Row 1: Using A, ch21.
Row 2: 1sc in 2nd ch from hook (missed ch does not count as sc), 1sc in each of next 2 ch, 1hdc in each of next 3 ch, 1dc in each of next 8 ch, 1hdc in each of next 3 ch, 1sc in each of next 3 ch. (20 sts)
Row 3: Ch1 (counts as first sc), 1scBLO in each of next 2 sc, 1hdcBLO in each of next 3 hdc, 1dcBLO in each of next 8 dc, 1hdcBLO in each of next 3 hdc, 1scBLO in each of next 3 sc.
Rows 4–27: Repeat Row 3.
Fasten off.

HEAD
Round 1: Using two strands of B held together, ch4, join with a sl st to form a ring.
Round 2: Ch1 (counts as first sc), 7sc in ring, join with a sl st. (8 sts)
Round 3: Ch1, 1sc in same sc, [2sc in next sc] to end, join with a sl st. (16 sts)
Round 4: Ch1, 2sc in next sc, [1sc in next sc, 2sc in next sc] to end, join with a sl st. (24 sts)
Round 5: Ch1, 1sc in next sc, 2sc in next sc, [1sc in each of next 2 sc, 2sc in next sc] to end, join with a sl st. (32 sts)
Round 6: Ch1, 1sc in each of next 2 sc, 2sc in next sc, [1sc in each of next 3 sc, 2sc in next sc] to end, join with a sl st. (40 sts)
Rounds 7–16: Ch1, 1sc in next sc, 1sc in each sc to end, join with a sl st.
Round 17: Ch1, 1sc in each of next 2 sc, sc2tog, [1sc in each of next 3 sc, sc2tog] to end, join with a sl st. (32 sts)
Round 18: Ch1, 1sc in next sc, 1sc in each sc to end, join with a sl st.

pomeranian pumpkin pal **89**

Round 19: Ch1, 1sc in next sc, sc2tog, [1sc in each of next 2 sc, sc2tog] to end, join with a sl st. (*24 sts*)
Round 20: Ch1, sc2tog, [1sc in next sc, sc2tog] to end, join with a sl st. (*16 sts*)
Fasten off.

SNOUT
Round 1: Using two strands of B held together, ch4, join with a sl st to form a ring.
Round 2: Ch1 (counts as first sc), 7sc in ring, join with a sl st. (*8 sts*)
Round 3: Ch1, 2sc in next sc, [1sc in next sc, 2sc in next sc] to end, join with a sl st. (*12 sts*)
Round 4: Ch1, 1sc in next sc, 1sc in each sc to end, join with a sl st.
Round 5: Ch1, 1sc in next sc, 2sc in next sc, [1sc in each of next 2 sc, 2sc in next sc] to end, join with a sl st. (*16 sts*)
Round 6: Ch1, 1sc in each of next 2 sc, 2sc in next sc, [1sc in each of next 3 sc, 2sc in next sc] to end, join with a sl st. (*20 sts*)
Rounds 7 and 8: Ch1, 1sc in next sc, 1sc in each sc to end, join with a sl st.
Fasten off B, join in two strands of C held together. Ch12, 1sc in 2nd ch from hook (missed ch does not count as sc), 1sc into each ch to end, sl st into next sc of Round 8 of snout.
Fasten off.

EARS
(make 2)
Round 1: Using two strands of B held together, ch4, join with a sl st to form a ring.
Round 2: Ch1 (counts as first sc), 7sc in ring, join with a sl st. (*8 sts*)
Round 3: Ch1, 1sc in same sc, [2sc in next sc] to end, join with a sl st. (*16 sts*)
Round 4: Ch1, 2sc in next sc, [1sc in next sc, 2sc in next sc] to last 4 sts, 1sc in next sc, leave remaining sts unworked, do not join. (*22 sts*)
Fasten off.

HAT
Round 1: Using D, ch4, join with a sl st to form a ring.
Round 2: Ch1 (counts as first sc), 7sc in ring, join with a sl st. (*8 sts*)
Round 3: Ch1, 1scBLO in next sc, 1scBLO in each sc to end.
Rounds 4-8: Ch1, 1sc in next sc, 1sc in each sc to end, join with a sl st.
Round 9: Ch13, 2sc in 2nd ch from hook (missed ch does not count as sc), 2sc in each ch to end (you have now worked back to main round), 1sc in same sc (at base of 13 ch), 2sc in each sc to end, join with a sl st. (*16 sts on main round*)
Round 10: Working on the main round only again, ch1, 2sc in next sc, [1sc in next sc, 2sc in next sc] to end, join with a sl st. (*24 sts*)
Round 11: Ch1, 1sc in next sc, 2sc in next sc, [1sc in each of next 2 sc, 2sc in next sc] to end, join with a sl st. (*32 sts*)
Fasten off.

ARMS AND LEGS
(make 4)
Round 1: Using two strands of B held together, ch4, join with a sl st to form a ring.
Round 2: Ch1 (counts as first sc), 9sc in ring, join with a sl st. (*10 sts*)
Rounds 3-12: Ch1, 1sc in next sc, 1sc in each sc to end, join with a sl st.
Fasten off.

decorative and cuddly dogs

TO MAKE UP

Sew the seam of the body together leaving a small opening. Stuff the body firmly to make a pumpkin shape, then sew the remainder of the seam.

Using E, embroider the mouth markings onto the snout (see page 141) using the photo as a guide. Add the safety nose and secure with the back (see page 141). Stuff the snout and sew it to the head, positioning the yarn C stripe so that it sits vertically up the center of the forehead.

Add the safety eyes to the head, using the photo as a guide for position, and secure with the backs. Stuff the head firmly and the sew the ears on either side. Sew the head to the body. Stuff the hat lightly and sew to the head.

Stuff the arms and legs and sew them to body using the photo as a guide for position.

Add the ladybug to the hat and the spider to the body and secure each with a few stitches.

pomeranian pumpkin pal 91

What more could any Westie owner ask for with this luxuriously soft cuddle pal? Worked with two strands of yarn held together to give the extra furry feel, using single crochet stitch throughout, this is a perfect gift for any dog lover.

west highland terrier cuddle pal

SKILL RATING ● ● ●

YARN AND MATERIALS
King Cole Luxury Fur (90% nylon, 10% polyester), worsted (Aran) weight yarn, 100yd (92m) per 3½oz (100g) ball
  3 balls of White 4200 (A)

Small amount of pink bulky (chunky) weight yarn (B)

Small amount of black light worsted (DK) weight yarn (C)

1in (24mm) safety nose

Toy fiberfill

Pair of ¾in (20mm) safety eyes

Short length of ribbon (optional)

HOOK AND EQUIPMENT
US 7 (4.5mm) crochet hook

Stitch marker

Yarn needle

Stiff brush or pet brush

FINISHED SIZE
Approx. 16in (40.5cm) tall

ABBREVIATIONS
See page 142.

PATTERN NOTES
Yarn A is worked with two strands held together throughout. It is advisable to use a stitch marker with this pattern. Turn to the "wrong side," which is fluffier, for brushing before filling with fiberfill.
If giving the West Highland Terrier to a young child, substitute the safety nose and eyes with embroidery in black yarn (see page 141).

WEST HIGHLAND TERRIER
BODY
Round 1: Using two strands of A held together, ch4, join with a sl st to form a ring.
Round 2: Ch1 (counts as first sc), 11sc in ring, join with a sl st. (*12 sts*)
Round 3: Ch1, 1sc in same sc, [2sc in next sc] to end, join with a sl st. (*24 sts*)
Round 4: Ch1, 1sc in each of next 7 sc, [2sc in next sc] four times, 1sc in each of next 8 sc, [2sc in next sc] four times, join with a sl st. (*32 sts*)
Round 5: Ch1, 1sc in next sc, 1sc in each sc to end, join with a sl st.
Round 6: Ch1, 1sc in each of next 2 sc, 2sc in next sc, [1sc in each of next 3 sc, 2sc in next sc] to end, join with a sl st. (*40 sts*)
Round 7: Ch1, 1sc in next sc, 1sc in each sc to end, join with a sl st.
Round 8: Ch1, 1sc in each of next 3 sc, 2sc in next sc, [1sc in each of next 4 sc, 2sc in next sc] to end, join with a sl st. (*48 sts*)
Rounds 9-20: Ch1, 1sc in next sc, 1sc in each sc to end, join with a sl st.
Round 21: Ch1, 1sc in each of next 3 sc, sc2tog, [1sc in each of next 4 sc, sc2tog] to end, join with a sl st. (*40 sts*)
Rounds 22-24: Ch1, 1sc in next sc, 1sc in each sc to end, join with a sl st.
Round 25: Ch1, 1sc in each of next 2 sc, sc2tog, [1sc in each of next 3 sc, sc2tog] to end, join with a sl st. (*32 sts*)
Rounds 26-28: Ch1, 1sc in next sc, 1sc in each sc to end, join with a sl st.
Round 29: Ch1, 1sc in each of next 7 sc, [sc2tog] four times, 1sc in each of next 8 sc, [sc2tog] 4 times, join with a sl st. (*24 sts*)
Rounds 30 and 31: Ch1, 1sc in next sc, 1sc in each sc to end, join with a sl st.
Turn work inside out so that the "wrong side" is on the outside. Stuff firmly.
Round 32: [Sc2tog] to end, join with a sl st. (*12 sts*)
Fasten off, leaving a length of yarn.
Thread end onto needle and gather remaining sts together.

decorative and cuddly dogs

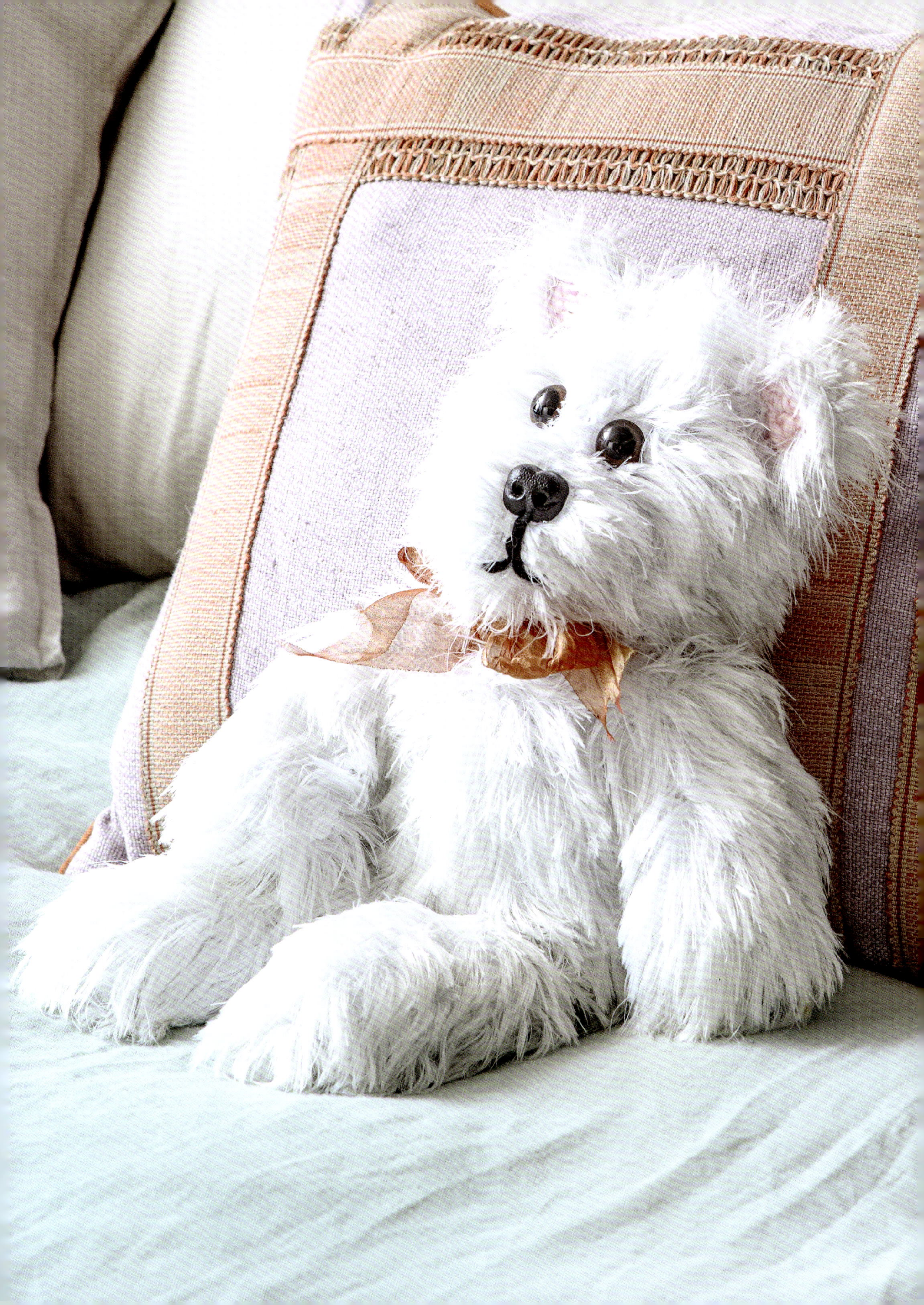

HEAD
Round 1: Using two strands of A held together, ch4, join with a sl st to form a ring.
Round 2: Ch1 (counts as first sc), 7sc in ring, join with a sl st. (*8 sts*)
Round 3: Ch1, 2sc in next sc, [1sc in next sc, 2sc in next sc] to end, join with a sl st. (*12 sts*)
Round 4: Ch1, 1sc in next sc, 1sc in each sc to end, join with a sl st.
Round 5: Ch1, 2sc in next sc, [1sc in next sc, 2sc in next sc] to end, join with a sl st. (*18 sts*)
Rounds 6-9: Ch1, 1sc in next sc, 1sc in each sc to end, join with a sl st.
Round 10: Ch1, 1sc in next sc, 2sc in next sc, [1sc in each of next 2 sc, 2sc in next sc] to end, join with a sl st. (*24 sts*)
Round 11: Ch1, 2sc in next sc, [1sc in next sc, 2sc in next sc] to end, join with a sl st. (*36 sts*)
Round 12: Ch1, 1sc in next sc, 1sc in each sc to end, join with a sl st.
Round 13: Ch1, 1sc in next sc, 2sc in next sc, [1sc in each of next 2 sc, 2sc in next sc] to end, join with a sl st. (*48 sts*)
Rounds 14-19: Ch1, 1sc in next sc, 1sc in each sc to end, join with a sl st.
Round 20: Ch1, 1sc in next sc, sc2tog, [1sc in each of next 2 sc, sc2tog] to end, join with a sl st. (*36 sts*)
Round 21: Ch1, sc2tog, [1sc in next sc, sc2tog] to end, join with a sl st. (*24 sts*)
Round 22: Ch1, 1sc in next sc, 1sc in each sc to end, join with a sl st.
Fasten off.
Turn work inside out so that the "wrong side" is on the outside.

SNOUT
Round 1: Using two strands of A held together, ch4, join with a sl st to form a ring.
Round 2: Ch1 (counts as first sc), 7sc in ring, join with a sl st. (*8 sts*)
Round 3: Ch1, 1sc in same sc, [2sc in next sc] to end, join with a sl st. (*16 sts*)
Round 4: Ch1, 1sc in each of next 2 sc, 2sc in next sc, [1sc in each of next 3 sc, 2sc in next sc] to end, join with a sl st. (*20 sts*)
Rounds 5-8: Ch1, 1sc in next sc, 1sc in each sc to end, join with a sl st.
Fasten off.
Turn work inside out so that the "wrong side" is on the outside.

INNER EARS
(make 2)
Row 1: Using B, ch2, 1sc in 2nd ch from hook (missed ch does not count as sc). (*1 st*)
Row 2: Ch1 (counts as first sc), 1sc in same st. (*2 sts*)
Row 3: Ch1, 1sc in same st, 1sc in each sc to end. (*3 sts*)
Row 4: Ch1, 1sc in same st, 1sc in each sc to end. (*4 sts*)
Row 5: Ch1, 1sc in same st, 1sc in each sc to end. (*5 sts*)
Row 6: Ch1, 1sc in same st, 1sc in each sc to end. (*6 sts*)
Fasten off.

OUTER EARS
(make 2)
Row 1: Using two strands of A held together, ch2, 1sc in 2nd ch from hook (missed ch does not count as sc). (*1 st*)
Row 2: Ch1 (counts as first sc), 1sc in same st. (*2 sts*)
Row 3: Ch1, 1sc in same st, 1sc in each sc to end. (*3 sts*)
Row 4: Ch1, 1sc in same st, 1sc in each sc to end. (*4 sts*)
Row 5: Ch1, 1sc in same st, 1sc in each sc to end. (*5 sts*)
Row 6: Ch1, 1sc in same st, 1sc in each sc to end. (*6 sts*)
Fasten off.

ARMS
(make 2)
Round 1: Using two strands of A held together, ch4, join with a sl st to form a ring.
Round 2: Ch1 (counts as first sc), 7sc in ring, join with a sl st. (*8 sts*)

Round 3: Ch1, 2sc in next sc, [1sc in next sc, 2sc in next sc] to end, join with a sl st. (*12 sts*)
Round 4: Ch1, 1sc in next sc, 1sc in each sc to end, join with a sl st.
Round 5: Ch1, 1sc in next sc, 2sc in next sc, [1sc in each of next 2 sc, 2sc in next sc] to end, join with a sl st. (*16 sts*)
Rounds 6-8: Ch1, 1sc in next sc, 1sc in each sc to end, join with a sl st.
Round 9: Ch1, 1sc in next sc, sc2tog, [1sc in each of next 2 sc, sc2tog] to end, join with a sl st. (*12 sts*)
Rounds 10-20: Ch1, 1sc in next sc, 1sc in each sc to end, join with a sl st.
Fasten off.
Turn work inside out so that the "wrong side" is on the outside.

LEGS
(make 2)
Round 1: Using two strands of A held together, ch4, join with a sl st to form a ring.
Round 2: Ch1 (counts as first sc), 9sc in ring, join with a sl st. (*10 sts*)
Round 3: Ch1, 1sc in each of next 2 sc, [2sc in next sc] twice, 1sc in each of next 3 sc, [2sc in next sc] twice, join with a sl st. (*14 sts*)
Round 4: Ch1, 1sc in each of next 4 sc, [2sc in next sc] twice, 1sc in each of next 5 sc, [2sc in next sc] twice, join with a sl st. (*18 sts*)
Round 5: Ch1, 1sc in each of next 6 sc, [2sc in next sc] twice, 1sc in each of next 7 sc, [2sc in next sc] twice, join with a sl st. (*22 sts*)
Rounds 6 and 7: Ch1, 1sc in next sc, 1sc in each sc to end, join with a sl st.
Round 8: Ch1, sc2tog, [1sc, sc2tog] three times, 1sc in each sc to end, join with a sl st. (*18 sts*)
Round 9: Ch1, sc2tog, [1sc, sc2tog] twice, 1sc in each sc to end, join with a sl st. (*15 sts*)
Rounds 10-22: Ch1, 1sc in next sc, 1sc in each sc to end, join with a sl st.
Round 23: Ch1, sc2tog, [1sc, sc2tog] three times, 1sc in each sc to end, join with a sl st. (*18 sts*)
Round 24: Ch1, sc2tog, [1sc, sc2tog] twice, 1sc in each sc to end, join with a sl st. (*15 sts*)
Fasten off.
Turn work inside out so that the "wrong side" is on the outside.

TO MAKE UP
Stuff the head firmly.

Using C, embroider the mouth markings onto the snout (see page 141) using the photo as a guide. Insert the safety nose and secure with the back (see page 141). Stuff the snout firmly and sew to the head using the photo as a guide for position.

Add the safety eyes to the head using the photo as a guide for position, and secure with the backs.

Place an inner ear piece on top of an outer ear piece and, using two strands of A held together, work a single crochet seam around (see page 140), working through both layers to join pieces together. Sew the ears to the top of head.

Sew the head to the body. Stuff and then sew the arms and legs to the body, flattening the arm and leg openings.

Brush with a stiff brush or pet brush to give the fluffy look. Tie the ribbon in a bow around the neck for decoration (optional).

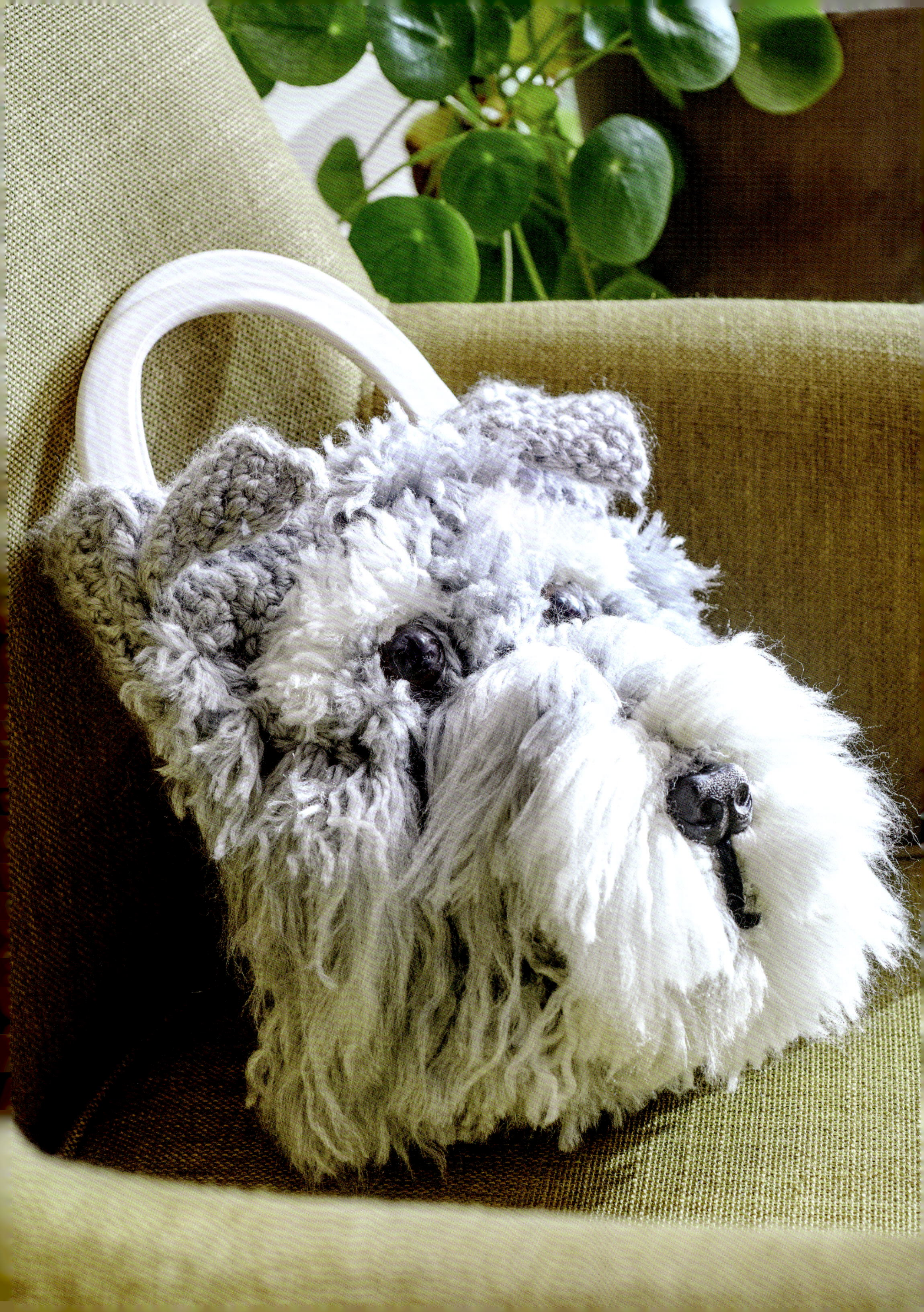

CHAPTER 4
bags and accessories

shih tzu purse

This charming little purse will be popular with all Shih Tzu lovers, with its pretty little face and ponytail. The front and back of the bag are worked in double crochet stitches in the main shade. The fur is created with a multitude of shades, and you can brush and trim it to the length required to create a likeness of your own pet.

SKILL RATING ● ● ○

YARN AND MATERIALS
King Cole Big Value Super Chunky (100% acrylic), super bulky (super chunky) weight yarn, 90yd (81m) per 3½oz (100g) ball
  3 balls of Latte 3490 (light brown) (A)

King Cole Quartz Super Chunky (90% acrylic, 10% wool), super bulky (super chunky) weight yarn, 92yd (85m) per 3½oz (100g) ball
  1 ball of Tiger's Eye 4471 (brown and cream) (B)

Small amount of black light worsted (DK) weight yarn (C)

1 3/16in (30mm) safety nose

Small amount of toy fiberfill

Pair of 1in (24mm) safety eyes

Small amount of ribbon (optional)

Hairspray (optional)

Pair of bamboo bag handles (or similar)

HOOK AND EQUIPMENT
US J-10 (6mm) crochet hook
Stitch marker
Yarn needle
Stiff brush or pet brush

FINISHED SIZE
Approx. 10in (25.5cm) square

ABBREVIATIONS
See page 142.

FRONT AND BACK
(make 2)
Row 1: Using A, ch33.
Row 2: 1dc in 4th ch from hook (missed 3 ch do not count as dc), 1dc in each ch to end. (*30 sts*)
Row 3: Ch3 (counts as first dc), [1FPdc around next dc, 1BPdc around next dc] to last dc, 1dc in last dc.
Repeat Row 3 until work measures approx. 10in (25.5cm).
Fasten off.

SNOUT
Round 1: Using A, ch4, join with a sl st to form a ring.
Round 2: Ch1 (counts as first sc), 7sc in ring, join with a sl st. (*8 sts*)
Round 3: Ch1, 1sc in same sc, [2sc in each sc] to end, join with a sl st. (*16 sts*)
Round 4: Ch1, 2sc in next sc, [1sc in next sc, 2sc in next sc] to end, join with a sl st. (*24 sts*)
Round 5: Ch1, 1sc in next sc, 2sc in next sc, [1sc in each of next 2 sc, 2sc in next sc] to end, join with a sl st. (*32 sts*)
Rounds 6–9: Ch1, 1sc in next sc, 1sc in each sc to end, join with a sl st.
Fasten off.

EYE POST COVER
(make 2)
To cover backs of eyes inside bag.
Row 1: Using A, ch13.
Row 2: 1sc in 2nd ch from hook (missed ch does not count as sc), 1sc in each ch to end. (*12 sts*)
Rows 3 and 4: Ch1, 1sc in next sc, 1sc in each sc to end.
Fasten off, leaving a length of yarn for sewing.

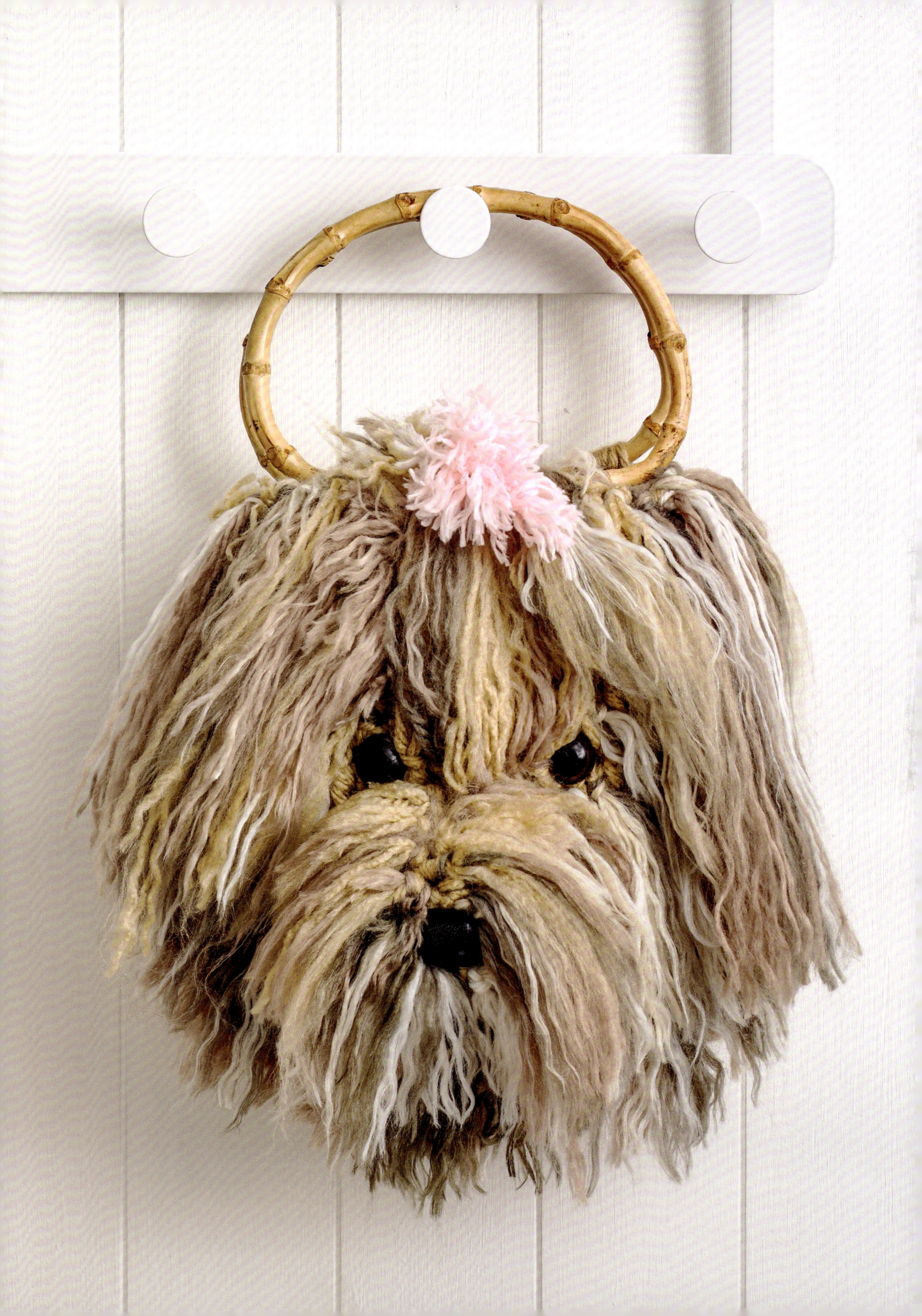

TO MAKE UP

Place the front of bag onto the back with right sides together. Using A, starting at top left corner, work a single crochet seam (see page 140) down one side, along the bottom and up the other side to join both pieces together, leaving the top open. Turn right side out.

Using C, embroider the mouth markings to the snout in positions required (see page 141), using the photo as a guide. Add the nose and secure with the safety back (see page 141). Stuff the snout and sew to the front of the bag.

Attach the safety eyes and then clip off the surplus eye posts. Sew the covers over the eye posts on the inside of the bag.

ADDING FUR

Adding the fur on the face can be done in two ways, either with a crochet hook (see page 141) or threading each strand through with a yarn needle and then tying the ends into a knot close to the fabric. The needle is better for getting into small areas, such as around the eyes. The fur is added to the front of the bag only, mixing the two colors as you prefer.

Snout

Cut lengths of A and B approx. 5in (12.5cm) long. Start at the top of the snout and work a row of fur fringing along it to the nose. Repeat on the other side of the snout. Work another row of fur fringing approx. 1in (2.5cm) below the first. Trim to the length required and brush for the "fluffy" effect.

Ponytail

Cut lengths of A and B approx. 12in (30cm) long. Starting at top of the snout, add a line of fur fringing between the eyes. Brush for the "fluffy" effect and trim to the length required. Gather and pull up to the forehead. Tie with a length of yarn and sew to the front of the bag. Add the ribbon in a bow (optional).

Rest of face

Continue using the 5in (12.5cm) lengths to cover the rest of the face and under the snout, working the rows approx. 2in (5cm) apart. Brush and trim in line with the bottom of the purse.

It may be beneficial to spray with hairspray to keep the yarn in place (optional).

Sew the handles on either side of the bag opening in a suitable position.

terrier large tote bag

This bag would look very fashionable wherever you take it. Created in a very soft purple shade with two cheeky little Terriers on the front, it's perfect for any occasion. The bag is worked in double crochet stitch and the dogs are made with single crochet stitch.

SKILL RATING ● ● ●

YARN AND MATERIALS
King Cole Big Value Super Chunky (100% acrylic), super bulky (super chunky) weight yarn, 90yd (81m) per 3½oz (100g) ball
  4 balls of Amethyst 3554 (purple) (A)

King Cole Luxury Fur (90% nylon, 10% polyester), worsted (Aran) weight yarn, 100yd (92m) per 3½oz (100g) ball
  ½ ball each of:
  Beaver 4208 (dark gray and white) (B)
  Wolf 4213 (off-white) (C)

Small amount of black light worsted (DK) weight yarn (D)

Pair of ¾in (20mm) safety noses

Small amount of toy fiberfill

2 pairs of ¾in (18mm) safety eyes

Hairspray (optional)

HOOKS AND EQUIPMENT
US J-10 (6mm) and US H-8 (5mm) crochet hooks

Stitch marker

Pins

Yarn needle

Stiff brush or pet brush

FINISHED SIZE
Approx. 16 x 13in (40 x 33cm) (not including handles)

ABBREVIATIONS
See page 142.

PATTERN NOTES
Luxury Fur is worked with two strands of yarn held together. It is advisable to use a stitch marker.

BAG FRONT AND BACK
(make 2)
Row 1: Using a US J-10 (6mm) hook and A, ch42.
Row 2: 1dc in 3rd ch from hook (missed 2 ch does not count as dc), 1dc in each ch to end. (*40 sts*)
Rows 3–19: Ch3 (counts as first dc), 1dc in next dc, 1dc in each dc to end.
Fasten off.

HANDLES
(make 2)
Row 1: Using a US J-10 (6mm) hook and A, ch11.
Row 2: 1sc in 2nd ch from hook (missed ch does not count as sc), 1sc in each ch to end. (*10 sts*)
Rows 3–40: Ch1 (counts as first sc), 1sc in next sc, 1sc in each sc to end.
Fasten off, leaving a length of yarn for sewing.

DOG

HEAD
(make 2)
Row 1: Using a US H-8 (5mm) hook and two strands of B held together, ch15.
Row 2: 1sc in 2nd ch from hook (missed ch does not count as sc), 1sc in each sc to end. (*14 sts*)
Row 3: Ch1 (counts as first sc), 1sc in next sc, 1sc in each sc to end.
Row 4: Ch1, 1sc in same sc, 1sc in each sc to last st, 2sc in last sc. (*16 sts*)
Row 5: Ch1, 1sc in next sc, 1sc in each sc to end.
Row 6: Ch1, 2sc in next sc, [1sc in next sc, 2sc in next sc] to end. (*24 sts*)
Row 7: Ch1, 1sc in next sc, 1sc in each sc to end.
Row 8: Ch1, 1sc in next sc, 2sc in next sc, [1sc in each of next 2 sc, 2sc in next sc] to end, join with a sl st. (*32 sts*)
Rows 9–21: Ch1, 1sc in next sc, 1sc in each sc to end.
Row 22: Sc2tog, 1sc in each sc to last 2 sts, sc2tog. (*30 sts*)
Fasten off.

SNOUT
(make 2)
Round 1: Using a US H-8 (5mm) hook and two strands of C held together, ch4, join with a sl st to form a ring.
Round 2: Ch1 (counts as first sc), 7sc in ring, join with a sl st. (*8 sts*)
Round 3: Ch1, 2sc in next sc, [1sc in next sc, 2sc in next sc] to end, join with a sl st. (*12 sts*)
Round 4: Ch1, 1sc in next sc, 1sc in each sc to end, join with a sl st.
Round 5: Ch1, 1sc in next sc, 2sc in next sc, [1sc in each of next 2 sc, 2sc in next sc] to end, join with a sl st. (*16 sts*)
Round 6: Ch1, 1sc in each of next 2 sc, 2sc in next sc, [1sc in each of next 3 sc, 2sc in next sc] to end, join with a sl st. (*20 sts*)
Rounds 7 and 8: Ch1, 1sc in next sc, 1sc in each sc to end, join with a sl st.
Fasten off.

EARS
(make 4)
Round 1: Using a US H-8 (5mm) hook and two strands of B held together, ch4, join with a sl st to form a ring.
Round 2: Ch1 (counts as first sc), 7sc in ring, join with a sl st. (*8 sts*)
Round 3: Ch1, 1sc in next sc, 1sc in each sc to end, join with a sl st.
Round 4: Ch1, 2sc in next sc, [1sc in next sc, 2sc in next sc] to end, join with a sl st. (*12 sts*)
Rounds 5 and 6: Ch1, 1sc in next sc, 1sc in each sc to end, join with a sl st.
Fasten off.

PAWS
(make 4)
Row 1: Using a US H-8 (5mm) hook and two strands of B held together, ch7.
Row 2: 1sc in 2nd ch from hook (missed ch does not count as sc), 1sc in each sc to end. (*6 sts*)
Rows 3–9: Ch1 (counts as first sc), 1sc in next sc, 1sc in each sc to end.
Fasten off.

TO MAKE UP
Place back and front pieces together with right sides facing. Using A, work a single crochet seam (see page 140) around the sides and bottom of the bag leaving the top open. Turn right side out.

Fold the handle in half widthwise and sew both edges together to give a thicker and sturdier strap. Sew a handle to the top of the bag at the back and the front.

DOG APPLIQUÉS
Using D, sew stitches for the mouth on the snout (see page 141), using the photograph as a guide. Insert a safety nose on each snout and add the back to secure (see page 141). Stuff each snout and sew one to each head in the position required. Add a pair of safety eyes on each dog face, using the photo as a guide for position, and secure with the backs.

Pin the heads to the front of the bag, using the photo as a guide for position, then sew in place. Fold each ear in half and sew the open end closed. Sew each pair of ears above a head, using the photo as a guide for position. Pin a pair of paws below the head and sew in place.

Brush each head to give the fluffy effect. Spray with hairspray to keep the fur in place (optional).

terrier large tote bag

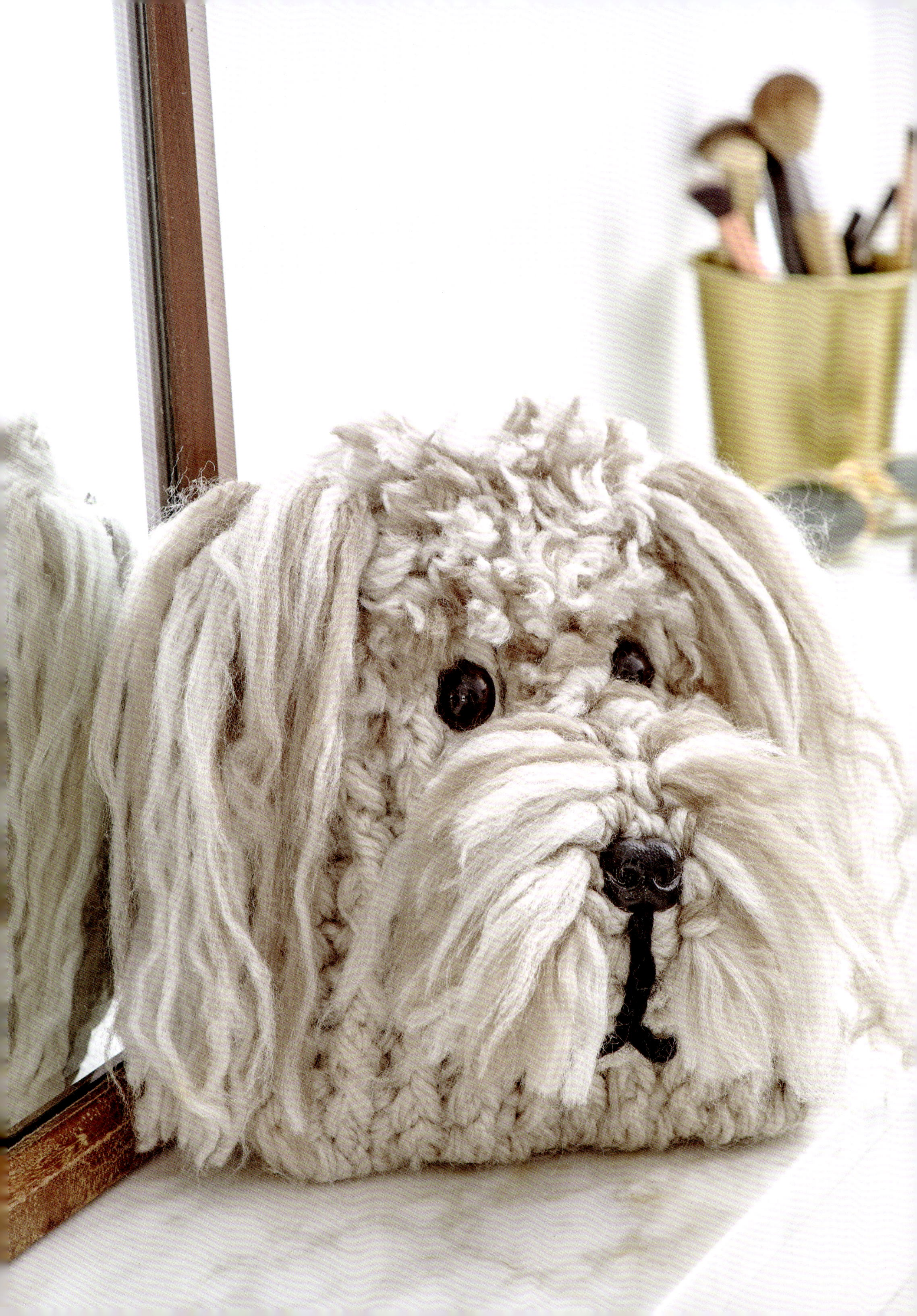

labradoodle makeup/clutch bag

What a perfect little clutch bag to take to a party to stand out from the crowd. With its fluffy face and a metal clasp to close, this pretty design is crocheted in single and double crochet stitches. You could make this pattern in different shades of yarn to resemble your favorite canine friend.

SKILL RATING ● ● ●

YARN AND MATERIALS
King Cole Big Value Super Chunky (100% acrylic), super bulky (super chunky) weight yarn, 90yd (81m) per 3½oz (100g) ball
- 2 balls of Oatmeal 14 (A)
- ½ ball of Gray 24 (B)

Small amount of black light worsted (DK) weight yarn (C)

1in (24mm) safety nose

Small amount of toy fiberfill

Pair of ¾in (20mm) safety eyes

Hairspray (optional)

6in (15.5cm) purse frame

HOOK AND EQUIPMENT
US H-8 (5mm) crochet hook

Yarn needle

Stiff brush or pet brush

Stitch marker

FINISHED SIZE
Approx. 6 x 7in (15.5 x 18cm)

ABBREVIATIONS
See page 142.

FRONT AND BACK
(make 2)
Row 1: Using A, ch25.
Row 2: 1dc in 3rd ch from hook (missed 2 ch does not count as dc), 1dc in each ch to end. (*23 sts*)
Row 3: Ch3 (counts as first dc), [1FPdc in next dc, 1BPdc in next dc] to last 2 dc, 1FPdc in next dc, 1dc in last dc.
Row 4: Ch3, [1BPdc in next dc, 1FPdc in next dc] to last 2 dc, 1BPdc in next dc, 1dc in last dc.
Repeat Rows 3 and 4 until work measures approx. 7in (18cm).
Fasten off.

SNOUT
Round 1: Using A, ch4, join with a sl st to form a ring.
Round 2: Ch1 (counts as first sc), 7sc in ring, join with a sl st. (*8 sts*)
Round 3: Ch1, 1sc in same sc, [2 sc in next sc] to end, join with a sl st. (*16 sts*)
Round 4: Ch1, 1sc in next sc, 1sc in each sc to end, join with a sl st.
Round 5: Ch1, 2sc in next sc, [1sc in next sc, 2sc in next sc] to end, join with a sl st. (*24 sts*)
Rounds 6–8: Ch1, 1sc in next sc, 1sc in each sc to end, join with a sl st.
Fasten off, leaving a length of yarn for sewing to front of bag.

EYE POST COVER
To cover backs of both eyes inside bag.
Row 1: Using A, ch10.
Row 2: 1sc in 2nd ch from hook (missed ch does not count as sc), 1sc in each ch to end. (*9 sts*)
Rows 3 and 4: Ch1 (counts as first sc), 1 sc in next sc, 1sc in each sc to end.
Fasten off, leaving a length of yarn for sewing to inside of bag.

TO MAKE UP

Place back and front pieces together with right sides facing. Using A, work a single crochet seam (see page 140) around the sides and bottom leaving the top edge and approx. 1in (2.5cm) from the top on each side open. Turn right side out.

Using C, sew long stitches for the mouth onto the snout (see page 141), using the photo as a guide. Add the safety nose in the position required and secure with the back (see page 141). Stuff the snout and sew to the bag using the photo as a guide for position.

Attach the safety eyes above the snout and secure with the backs. Clip off the surplus eye posts and then sew the cover for the back of the eyes onto the inside of the bag to cover the eye posts.

ADDING FUR

Adding the fur on the face can be done in two ways, either with a crochet hook (see page 141) or threading each strand through with a yarn needle and then tying the ends into a knot close to the fabric. The needle is better for getting into small areas, such as around the eyes.

Ears

Cut A and B into approx. 10in (25cm) lengths. Starting at the top of the bag add a short line of fur fringing to form the ear. Repeat on the other side of the bag. Trim to the length required and brush for the fluffy effect.

Snout

Cut A and B into approx. 5in (12.5cm) lengths. Add lines of fur fringing on both sides of the snout from the center to the tip of the nose. Trim to length required and brush for the fluffy effect.

Face

Cut A and B into approx. 5in (12.5cm) lengths. Add fur fringing above the nose and around the eyes to the top of the bag. Trim to length required and brush for the fluffy effect. Spray with hairspray to keep the fur in place (optional).

Sew the top edges of the bag to the purse frame.

maltese terrier purse

The Maltese Terrier is a gentle, affectionate little dog with a very pretty face which is replicated in this crochet purse. This bag is made in double crochet stitch with super bulky yarn, and then the fur is added to give the super-soft fluffy look.

SKILL RATING ●●○

YARN AND MATERIALS
King Cole Big Value Super Chunky (100% acrylic), super bulky (super chunky) weight yarn, 90yd (81m) per 3½oz (100g) ball
- 4 balls of Brown 31 or Champagne 12 (white) (A)

Small amount of black light worsted (DK) weight yarn (B)

1³⁄₁₆in (30mm) safety nose

Small amount of toy fiberfill

Pair of 1in (24mm) safety eyes

Hairspray (optional)

Pair of bag handles

HOOK AND EQUIPMENT
US J-10 (6mm) crochet hook

Yarn needle

Stiff brush or pet brush

Stitch marker

FINISHED SIZE
Approx. 11 x 11in (28 x 28cm)

ABBREVIATIONS
See page 142.

FRONT AND BACK OF BAG
(make 2)
Row 1: Using A, ch37.
Row 2: 1dc in 3rd ch from hook (missed 2 ch do not count as dc), 1dc in each ch to end. (35 sts)
Row 3: Ch3 (counts as first dc), [1FPdc in next dc, 1BPdc in next dc] to last 2 dc, 1FPdc in next dc, 1dc in last dc.
Row 4: Ch3, [1BPdc in next dc, 1FPdc in next dc] to last 2 dc, 1BPdc in next dc, 1dc in last dc.
Repeat Rows 3 and 4 until work measures approx. 11in (28cm).
Fasten off.

SNOUT
Round 1: Using A, ch4, join with a sl st to form a ring.
Round 2: Ch1 (counts as first sc), 7sc in ring, join with a sl st. (8 sts)
Round 3: Ch1, 1sc in same sc, [2sc in next sc] to end, join with a sl st to first sc. (16 sts)
Round 4: Ch1, 2sc in next sc, [1sc in next sc, 2sc in next sc] to end, join with a sl st. (24 sts)
Rounds 5-9: Ch1, 1sc in next sc, 1sc in each sc to end, join with a sl st.
Fasten off.

EYE POST COVER
To cover backs of eyes inside bag.
Row 1: Using A, ch13.
Row 2: 1sc in 2nd ch from hook (missed ch does not count as sc), 1sc in each ch to end. (12 sts)
Rows 3 and 4: Ch1 (counts as first sc), 1sc in next sc, 1sc in each sc to end.
Fasten off.

bags and accessories

TO MAKE UP
Place back and front pieces together with right sides facing. Using A, work a single crochet seam around the sides and bottom of the bag leaving the top edge open. Turn right side out.

Using B, sew long stitches for the mouth onto the snout, using the photo as a guide. Attach the safety nose in position and secure with the back. Stuff the snout and sew to the bag using the photo as a guide for position.

Add the safety eyes above the snout, using the photo as a guide for position, and secure with the backs. Clip off the surplus eye posts and sew the cover for the backs of the eyes onto the inside of the bag to cover the eye posts.

ADDING FUR
Adding the fur on the face can be done in two ways, either with a crochet hook (see page 141) or threading each strand through with a yarn needle and then tying the ends into a knot close to the fabric. The needle is better for getting into small areas, such as around the eyes.

Ears
Cut A into approx. 10in (25cm) lengths. Starting at the top of the bag add a short length of fur fringing along one side to form the ear. Make a second line underneath. Repeat on the other side of the bag. Trim to the length required and brush for the fluffy effect—to produce fluffier ears more yarn can be added and brushed.

Snout
Cut A into approx. 7in (18cm) lengths. Add lines of fur fringing of yarn on both sides of the snout from the center to the tip of the snout. Trim to the length required and brush for the fluffy effect—for a fluffier snout, more yarn can be added and brushed.

Face
Cut A into approx. 5in (12.5cm) lengths. Add lines of fur fringing above the snout and around the eyes to the top of the bag, approx. 1in (2.5cm) apart. The closer the lines, the fluffier the dog will be. Continue to add fur fringing until all spaces are filled in. Trim to length required and brush for the fluffy effect.

Spray with hairspray to keep the yarn in place (optional).

Sew the handles in position.

This charming tote bag will turn heads wherever you go. The soft, long fur mimics the cheeky look of the popular Cockapoo's super-fluffy face. Both sides of the purse are crocheted in double crochet stitches, covered with brushed wool, while the snout and handles are worked in single crochet.

cockapoo purse

SKILL RATING ● ● ○

YARN AND MATERIALS
King Cole Big Value Super Chunky (100% acrylic), super bulky (super chunky) weight yarn, 90yd (81m) per 3½oz (100g) ball
  6 balls of Champagne 12 (white) (A)

Small amount of black bulky (chunky) weight yarn (B)

1 3/16 in (30mm) safety nose

Toy fiberfill

Pair of 1in (24mm) safety eyes

HOOK AND EQUIPMENT
US J-10 (6mm) crochet hook
Stitch marker
Yarn needle
Stiff brush or pet brush

FINISHED SIZE
Approx. 12 x 16in (30 x 40cm)

ABBREVIATIONS
See page 142.

BAG FRONT AND BACK
(make 2)
Row 1: Using A, ch34.
Row 2: 1dc in 3rd ch from hook (missed 2 ch do not count as dc), 1dc in each ch to end. (*32 sts*)
Rows 3–17: Ch3 (counts as first dc), 1dc in next dc, 1dc in each dc to end.
Fasten off.

EYE POST COVER
To cover backs of both eyes inside bag.
Row 1: Using A, ch19.
Row 2: 1sc in 2nd ch from hook (missed ch does not count as sc), 1sc in each ch to end. (*18 sts*)
Rows 3 and 4: Ch1 (counts as first sc), 1sc in next sc, 1sc in each sc to end.
Fasten off, leaving a length of yarn for sewing inside bag.

SNOUT
Round 1: Using A, ch4, join with a sl st to form a ring.
Round 2: Ch1 (counts as first sc), 7sc in ring, join with a sl st. (*8 sts*)
Round 3: Ch1, 1sc in same sc, [2sc in next sc] to end, join with a sl st. (*16 sts*)
Round 4: Ch1, 1sc in next sc, 1sc in each sc to end, join with a sl st. (*16 sts*)
Round 5: Ch1, 2sc in next sc, [1sc in next sc, 2sc in next sc] to end, join with a sl st. (*24 sts*)
Rounds 6 and 7: Ch1, 1sc in next sc, 1sc in each sc to end, join with a sl st.
Round 8: Ch1, 1sc in next sc, 2sc in next sc, [1sc in each of next 2 sc, 2sc in next sc] to end, join with a sl st. (*32 sts*)
Rounds 9 and 10: Ch1, 1sc in next sc, 1sc in each sc to end, join with a sl st.
Fasten off, leaving length of yarn for sewing to bag.

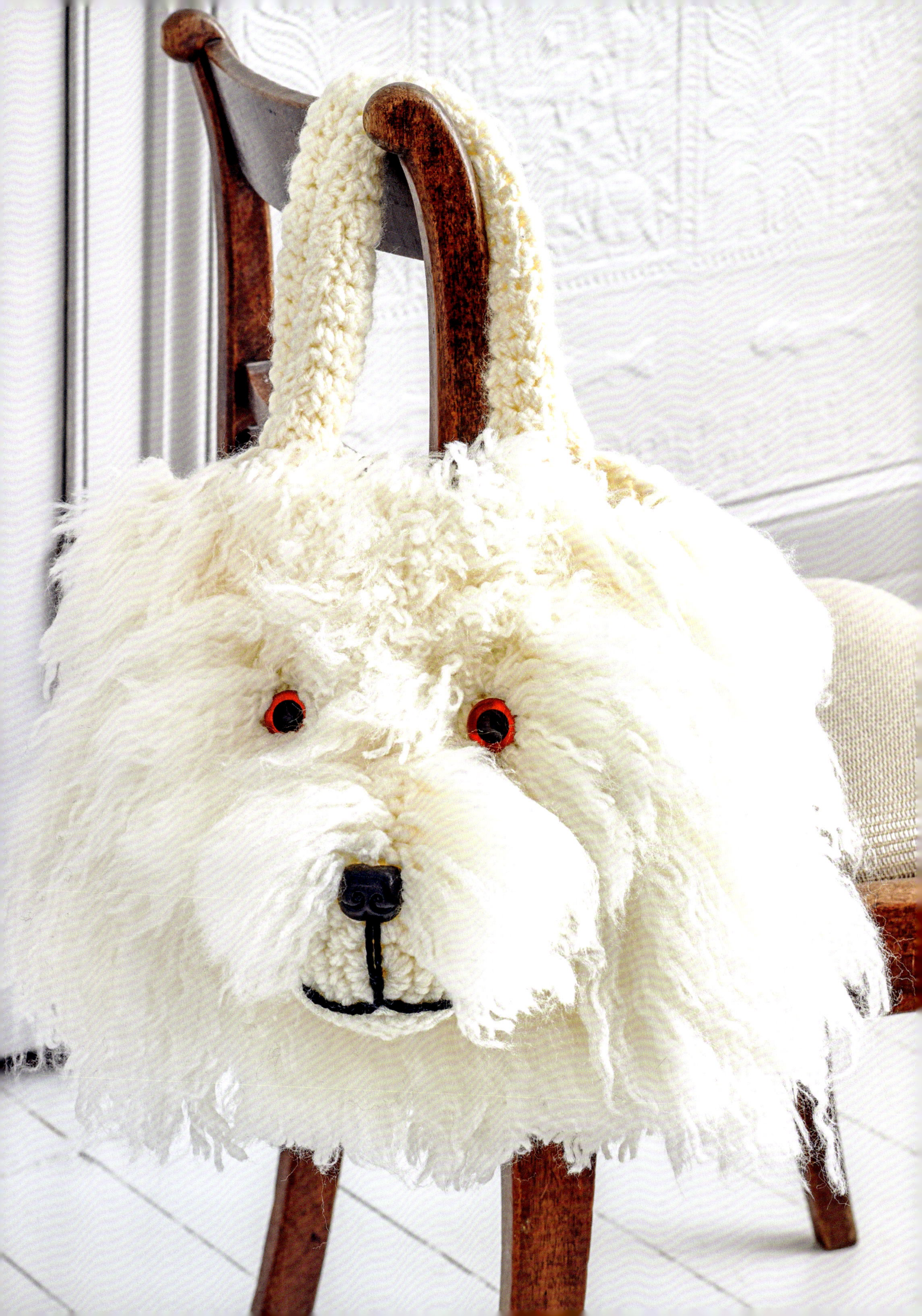

HANDLES
(make 2)
Row 1: Using A, ch11.
Row 2: 1sc in 2nd ch from hook (missed ch does not count as sc), 1sc in each ch to end. (*10 sts*)
Rows 3-36: Ch1 (counts as first sc), 1sc in next sc, 1sc in each sc to end.
Fasten off.
For longer handles add more rows if required.

TO MAKE UP
Place front and back with right sides together. Using A, work a single crochet seam (see page 140) around the sides and bottom, leaving the top edge open. Turn right side out.

Using B, embroider the mouth markings to the snout in positions required (see page 141), using the photo as a guide. Insert the safety nose and secure with the back (see page 141). Stuff the snout and sew to the front of the bag.

Attach the safety eyes and then clip off the surplus eye posts. Sew the cover over the eye posts on the inside of the bag.

Fold one long edge of the handle to the middle, then fold the other long edge over to give three layers. Using A, working through all three layers, sew along one short edge of the handle, then sew along the open long edge to secure the three layers together, then sew along the second short edge. Repeat for the other handle. Sew the handles to either side of the bag opening, with the ends approx. 4in (10cm) apart.

ADDING FUR
Adding the fur on the face can be done in two ways, either with a crochet hook (see page 141) or threading each strand through the fabric with a yarn needle and then tying the ends into a knot close to the fabric. The needle is better for getting into small areas, such as around the eyes.

Back and front of bag
The fur is added to both sides of the bag, working the back of the bag first, then the front. Cut lengths of A approx. 7in (18cm) long. Starting approx. 3in (7.5cm) from the bottom of the bag, work a line of fur fringing across the bag. Work further rows of fringing approx. 2in (5cm) above the previous row until you reach the top of the bag. Brush with a stiff brush or pet brush to give the fluffy look. Trim to shape and level the fur around the bottom of the bag. Work the front of the bag in the same manner, working around the snout. Trim around the eyes as required.

Snout
Cut lengths of A approx. 5in (12.5cm) long. Start at the top of the snout and work along it to the nose. Repeat on the other side of the snout. Work another row of fur fringing approx. 1in (2.5cm) below the first. Trim to the length required and brush for the "fluffy" effect.

Lower face
Continue with the 5in (12.5cm) lengths of A to add some fur fringing under the snout. Brush and trim in line with the bottom of the bag.

Ears
Cut strands of A approx. 10in (25cm) long. Starting from the side of head, add fur fringing to form the ears for approx. 1in (2.5cm) across the bag and down the side of the bag. Brush to give the fluffy effect and trim to the length required.

poodle golf club covers

What a head turner at your next game of golf! This popular Poodle-look golf club cover is crocheted in super bulky yarn to give the thickness to protect your valuable golf equipment. The cover is worked in single crochet stitches to last longer and will fit most driver head sizes. The neck is crocheted in double crochet stitches, working in crochet ribbing to give enough firmness so it will stay on the club.

SKILL RATING ● ● ○

YARN AND MATERIALS
King Cole Tufty Super Chunky (100% polyester), super bulky (super chunky) weight yarn, 87yd (80m) per 7oz (200g) ball
  1 ball in Gray 2799 or White 2791 (A)
King Cole Big Value Super Chunky (100% acrylic), super bulky (super chunky) weight yarn, 90yd (81m) per 3½oz (100g) ball
  ½ ball in Gray 24 or White 1758 (B)
Small amount of bulky (chunky) yarn in a contrast color (C)
Small amount of black light worsted (DK) weight yarn (D)
1in (24mm) safety nose
Small amount of toy fiberfill
Pair of ⅝in (16mm) safety eyes
Embellishments of your choice

HOOK AND EQUIPMENT
US J-10 (6mm) crochet hook
Stitch marker
Yarn needle
Sewing needle and thread

FINISHED SIZE
Approx. 9in (23cm) tall, to fit all standard golf clubs

ABBREVIATIONS
See page 142.

PATTERN NOTES
It is advisable to use a stitch marker with this pattern. The head section is worked with wrong side facing to give a fluffier effect.

COVER

HEAD AND SHOULDERS
Work in rounds on wrong side.
Round 1: Using A, ch4, join with a sl st to form a ring.
Round 2: Ch1 (counts as first sc), 7sc in ring, join with a sl st. (*8 sts*)
Round 3: Ch1, 1sc in same sc, [2sc in next sc] to end, join with a sl st. (*16 sts*)
Round 4: Ch1, 2sc in next sc, [1sc in next sc, 2sc in next sc] to end, join with a sl st. (*24 sts*)
Round 5: Ch1, 1sc in next sc, 2sc in next sc, [1sc in each of next 2 sc, 2sc in next sc] to end, join with a sl st. (*32 sts*)
Rounds 6–10: Ch1, 1sc in next sc, 1sc in each sc to end, join with a sl st.
Round 11: Ch1, 1sc in next sc, [sc2tog] to last 2 sc, 1sc in each of last 2 sc, join with a sl st. (*18 sts*)
Round 12: Change to B, ch1, 1sc in next sc, 1sc in each sc to end, join with a sl st.
Round 13: Ch3 (counts as first dc), 1dc in next sc, 1dc in each sc to end, join with a sl st.

poodle golf club covers 113

Turn work right side out and cont working on right side from now on.
Rounds 14-21: Ch3, [1FPdc in next dc, 1BPdc in next dc] to last dc, 1FPdc in last dc, join with a sl st.
Fasten off.

SNOUT
Round 1: Using B, ch4, join with a st st to form a ring.
Round 2: Ch1 (counts as first sc), 7sc in ring, join with a sl st. (*8 sts*)
Round 3: Ch1, 1sc in same sc, [2sc in next sc] to end, join with a sl st. (*16 sts*)
Rounds 4-8: Ch1, 1sc in next sc, 1sc in each sc to end, join with a sl st.
Fasten off, leaving a length of yarn for sewing to main head.

EARS
(make 2)
Row 1: Using A, ch4.
Row 2: 1sc in 2nd ch from hook (missed ch does not count as sc), 1sc in each ch to end. (*3 sts*)
Row 3: Ch1 (counts as first sc), 1sc in next sc, 1sc in each sc to end.
Row 4: Ch1, 1sc in same sc, 1sc in each sc to end. (*4 sts*)
Row 5: Ch1, 1sc in same sc, 1sc in each sc to end. (*5 sts*)
Row 6: Ch1, 1sc in same sc, 1sc in each sc to end. (*6 sts*)
Rows 7-11: Ch1, 1sc in next sc, 1sc in each sc to end.
Fasten off.

COLLAR
Row 1: Using C, ch26.
Row 2: 1dc in 3rd ch from hook (missed 2 ch do not count as dc), 1dc in each ch to end. (*24 sts*)
Fasten off.

EYE POST COVER
To cover backs of both eyes inside.
Row 1: Using B, ch13.
Row 2: 1sc in 2nd ch from hook (missed ch does not count as sc), 1sc in each ch to end. (*12 sts*)
Rows 3 and 4: Ch1 (counts as first sc), 1sc in next sc, 1sc in each sc to end.
Fasten off, leaving a length of yarn for sewing inside.

TO MAKE UP
Before making up it may be advisable to stuff the cover to give the right shape to work with.

Using D, sew long stitches for the mouth onto the snout (see page 141). Attach the safety nose in the position required (see page 141), using the photo as a guide. Stuff the snout and then sew to the head.

Attach the safety eyes and then clip off the surplus eye posts. Sew the eye post cover over the eye posts on the inside of the cover. Sew the ears to the head using the photo as a guide. Sew the collar around the neck. Trim the fur to the length required.

Decorate with your chosen embellishments.

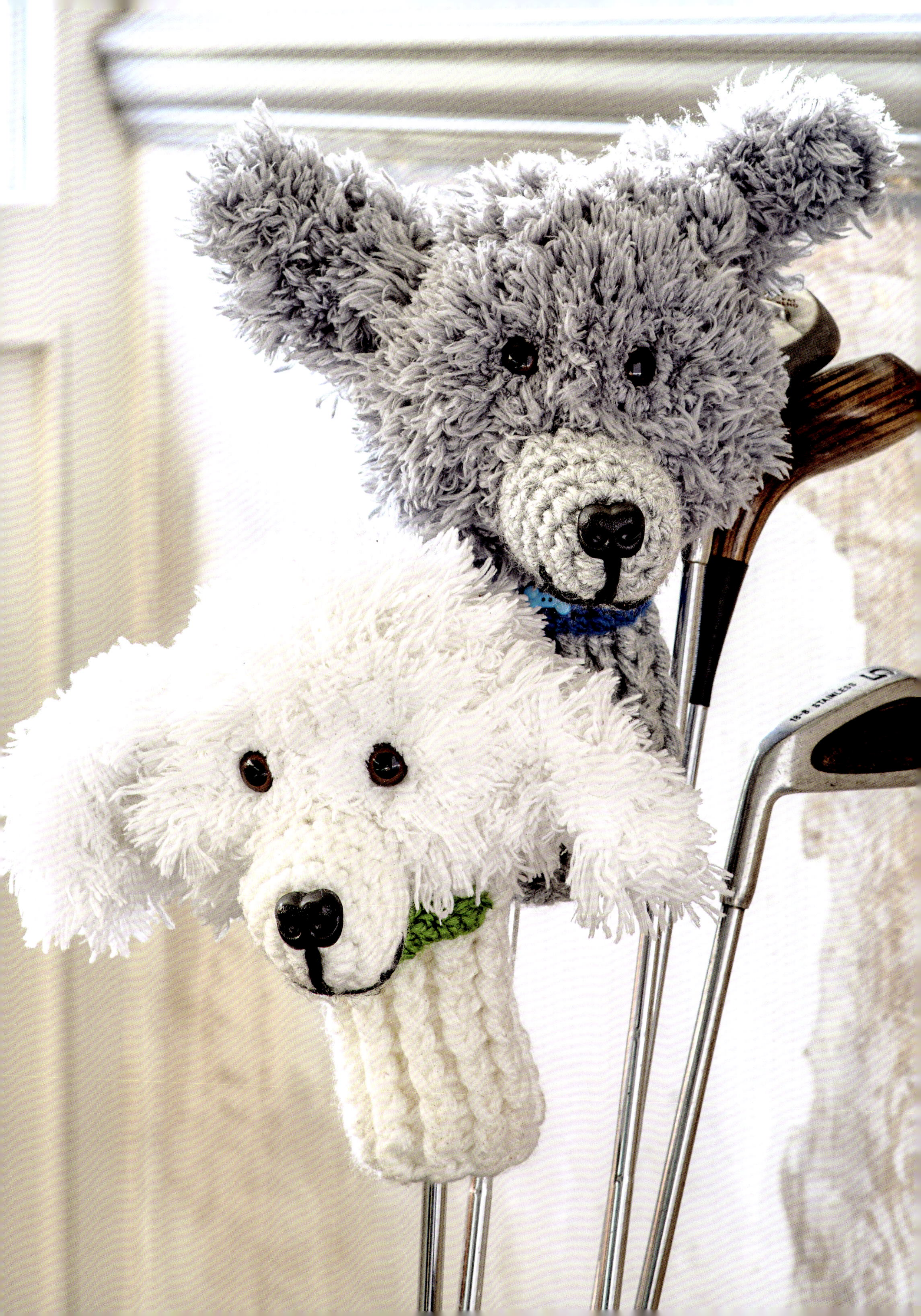

This trio of bags and coin purses would make a great gift for the Labrador lover. They are worked mainly in single crochet stitches, with some parts in double crochet stitches, using super bulky yarn for thickness and stability—making these a perfect project for the beginner.

chocolate labrador makeup bag and coin purses

SKILL RATING ● ○ ○

YARN AND MATERIALS
King Cole Big Value Super Chunky (100% acrylic), super bulky (super chunky) weight yarn, 90yd (81m) per 3½oz (100g) ball
  2½ balls of Chocolate 273 (brown) (A)
  Small amount of Black 8 (B)

1in (24mm) safety nose
¾in (20mm) safety nose
Small amount of toy fiberfill
Pair of ¾in (20mm) safety eyes
Pair of ½in (12mm) safety eyes

8in (20cm) zipper fastener
4in (10cm) zipper fastener
4in (10cm) purse frame
Embellishments for decoration

HOOK AND EQUIPMENT
US J-10 (6mm) crochet hook
Stitch marker
Yarn needle
Pins
Sewing needle and thread

FINISHED SIZES
Makeup bag   8 x 6½in (20 x 16.5cm)
Oblong coin purse   5 x 3½in (13 x 9cm)
Round coin purse   5 x 4in (13 x 10cm)

ABBREVIATIONS
See page 142.

116 bags and accessories

MAKEUP BAG
Row 1: Using A, ch23.
Row 2: 1sc in 2nd ch from hook (missed ch does not count as sc), 1sc in each ch to end. (*22 sts*)
Rows 3–40: Ch1 (counts as first sc), 1sc in next sc, 1sc in each sc to end.
Fasten off.

EYE POST COVER
To cover backs of both eyes inside bag.
Row 1: Using A, ch13.
Row 2: 1sc in 2nd ch from hook (missed ch does not count as sc), 1sc in each ch to end. (*12 sts*)
Rows 3 and 4: Ch1 (counts as first sc), 1sc in next sc, 1sc in each sc to end.
Fasten off, leaving a length of yarn.

SNOUT
Round 1: Using A, ch4, join with a sl st to form a ring.
Round 2: Ch1 (counts as first sc), 7sc in ring, join with a sl st. (*8 sts*)
Round 3: Ch1, 2sc in next sc, [1sc in next sc, 2sc in next sc] to end, join with a sl st. (*12 sts*)
Round 4: Ch1, 1sc in next sc, 2sc in next sc, [1sc in each of next 2 sc, 2sc in next sc] to end, join with a sl st. (*16 sts*)
Round 5: Ch1, 1sc in next sc, 1sc in each sc to end, join with a sl st.
Round 6: Ch1, 1sc in each of next 2 sc, 2sc in next sc, [1sc in each of next 3 sc, 2sc in next sc] to end, join with a sl st. (*20 sts*)
Rounds 7–10: Ch1, 1sc in next sc, 1sc in each sc to end, join with a sl st.
Fasten off.

EARS
(make 2)
Row 1: Using A, ch5.
Row 2: 1sc in 2nd ch from hook (missed ch does not count as sc), 1sc in each ch to end. (*4 sts*)
Row 3: Ch1 (counts as first sc), 1sc in same sc, 1sc in each sc to end. (*5 sts*)
Row 4: Ch1, 1sc in same sc, 1sc in each sc to end. (*6 sts*)
Rows 5 and 6: Ch1, 1sc in next sc, 1sc in each sc to end.
Row 7: Ch1, 1sc in same sc, 1sc in each sc to end. (*7 sts*)
Row 8: Ch1, 1sc in same sc, 1sc in each sc to end. (*8 sts*)
Rows 9 and 10: Ch1, 1sc in next sc, 1sc in each sc to end.
Row 11: Sc2tog, 1sc in each sc to last 2 sc, sc2tog. (*6 sts*)
Fasten off.

TO MAKE UP
Fold the main piece in half with right sides together. Using A, work a single crochet seam (see page 140) along each side edge. Turn right side out.

Using B, sew long stitches for the mouth onto the snout (see page 141). Add the 1in (24mm) safety nose using the photo as a guide for position and secure with the back (see page 141). Stuff the snout and sew to the front of the bag using the photo as a guide.

Attach the ¾in (20mm) eyes above the snout using the photo as a guide for position and secure with the back. Clip off the back of the eye stems and sew the eye post cover onto the inside of the bag to cover the eye stems.

Sew the ears to the bag, using the photo as a guide for position. Pin and then sew the 8in (20cm) zipper into place along the top of the bag, using the sewing needle and thread.

chocolate labrador makeup bag and coin purses

OBLONG COIN PURSE

Row 1: Using A, ch13.
Row 2: 1sc in 2nd ch from hook (missed ch does not count as sc), 1sc in each ch to end. (*12 sts*)
Rows 3-22: Ch1 (counts as first sc), 1sc in next sc, 1sc in each sc to end.
Fasten off.

TO MAKE UP

Fold the main piece in half with right sides together. Using A, work a single crochet seam (see page 140) along each side edge. Turn right side out.

Pin and then sew the 4in (10cm) zipper into place along the top of the bag, using the sewing needle and thread.

Add embellishments if required.

ROUND COIN PURSE

HEAD

(make 2)
Round 1: Using A, ch4, join with a sl st to form a ring.
Round 2: Ch3 (counts as first dc), 11dc in ring, join with a sl st. (*12 sts*)
Round 3: Ch3, 1dc in same dc, [2dc in next dc] to end, join with a sl st. (*24 sts*)
Round 4: Ch3, 2dc in next dc, [1dc in next dc, 2dc in next dc] five times, leave remaining sts unworked. (*18 sts*)
Fasten off.

SNOUT

Round 1: Using A, ch4, join with a sl st to form a ring.
Round 2: Ch1 (counts as first sc), 7sc in ring, join with a sl st. (*8 sts*)
Round 3: Ch1, 2sc in next sc, [1sc in next sc, 2sc in next sc] to end, join with a sl st. (*12 sts*)
Round 4: Ch1, 1sc in next sc, 1sc in each sc to end, join with a sl st.
Round 5: Ch1, 1sc in next sc, 2sc in next sc, [1sc in each of next 2 sc, 2sc in next sc] to end, join with a sl st. (*16 sts*)

Round 6: Ch1, 1sc in each of next 2 sc, 2sc in next sc, [1sc in each of next 3 sc, 2sc in next sc] to end, join with a sl st. (*20 sts*)
Rounds 7 and 8: Ch1, 1sc in next sc, 1sc in each sc to end, join with a sl st.
Fasten off.

EARS
(make 2)
Row 1: Using A, ch6.
Row 2: 1sc in 2nd ch from hook (missed ch does not count as sc), 1sc in each ch to end. (*5 sts*)
Rows 3-7: Ch1 (counts as first sc), 1sc in next sc, 1sc in each sc to end.
Row 8: Sc2tog, 1sc in next sc, sc2tog. (*3 sts*)
Fasten off.

EYE POST COVER
To cover backs of both eyes inside coin purse.
Row 1: Using A, ch9.
Row 2: 1sc in 2nd ch from hook (missed ch does not count as sc), 1sc in each ch to end. (*8 sts*)
Row 3: Ch1 (counts as first sc), 1sc in next sc, 1sc in each sc to end.
Fasten off, leaving a length of yarn.

TO MAKE UP
Place the front and back head pieces with right sides together, aligning the stitches worked in round 4. Using A, work a single crochet seam (see page 140) along the stitches worked in round 4, leaving the remaining section open (opening should measure approx. 4in/10cm). Turn right side out.

Using B, sew long stitches for the mouth onto the snout (see page 141). Add the ¾in (20mm) safety nose using the photo as a guide for position and secure with the back. Stuff the snout and sew to the front of the coin purse in the position required.

Attach the ½in (12mm) safety eyes above the snout using the photo as a guide for position and secure with the backs. Clip off the surplus eye posts and sew the covers over the eye posts on the inside of the bag.

Sew the ears to the coin purse, using the photo as a guide for position. Sew the frame into place along the top of the coin purse.

Add embellishments if required.

chocolate labrador makeup bag and coin purses

jack russell golf club cover

This smart little fellow will look perfect among your golf clubs with his bright little face. He is worked in single crochet stitches using a furry yarn with two strands at a time to give the extra thickness and stability.

SKILL RATING ● ● ○

YARN AND MATERIALS
King Cole Moments DK (100% polyester) light worsted (DK) weight yarn, 98yd (90m) per 1¾oz (50g) ball
  2 balls of Koala 499 (brown) (A)
  1 ball of White 470 (B)

King Cole Big Value Chunky (100% acrylic), bulky (chunky) weight yarn, 167yd (152m) per 3½oz (100g) ball
  Small amount of Turmeric 3486 (orange) (C)

Small amount of black light worsted (DK) weight yarn (D)

Small amount of toy fiberfill

Pair of ¾in (18mm) safety eyes

¾in (20mm) safety nose

Bone embellishment (optional)

HOOK AND EQUIPMENT
US 7 (4.5mm) crochet hook
Stitch marker
Yarn needle
Sewing needle and thread (optional)

FINISHED SIZE
Approx. 10in (25.5cm) tall

ABBREVIATIONS
See page 142.

PATTERN NOTES
The yarn is worked with two strands held together throughout.
It is advisable to use a stitch marker with this pattern.

COVER

HEAD AND SHOULDERS
Round 1: Using two strands of A held together, ch4, join with a sl st to form a ring.
Round 2: Ch1 (counts as first sc), 7sc in ring, join with sl st. (*8 sts*)
Round 3: Ch1, 1sc in same sc, [2sc in next sc] to end, join with a sl st. (*16 sts*)
Round 4: Ch1, 2sc in next sc, [1sc in next sc, 2sc in next sc] to end, join with a sl st. (*24 sts*)
Round 5: Ch1, 1sc in next sc, 2sc in next sc, [1sc in each of next 2 sc, 2sc in next sc] to end, join with a sl st. (*32 sts*)
Round 6: Ch1, 1sc in next sc, 1sc in each sc to end, join with a sl st.
Round 7: Ch1, 1sc in each of next 2 sc, 2sc in next sc, [1sc in each of next 3 sc, 2sc in next sc] to end, join with a sl st. (*40 sts*)
Round 8: Ch1, 1sc in next sc, 1sc in each sc to end, join with a sl st.
Round 9: Ch1, 1sc in each of next 3 sc, 2sc in next sc, [1sc in each of next 4 sc, 2sc in next sc] to end, join with a sl st. (*48 sts*)
Rounds 10-20: Ch1, 1sc in next sc, 1sc in each sc to end, join with a sl st.
Round 21: Ch1, 1sc in each of next 3 sc, sc2tog, [1sc in each of next 4 sc, sc2tog] to end, join with a sl st. (*40 sts*)
Rounds 22-25: Ch1, 1sc in next sc, 1sc in each sc to end, join with a sl st.
Round 26: Ch1, 1sc in next sc, sc2tog, [1sc in each of next 2 sc, sc2tog] to end, join with a sl st. (*30 sts*)
Rounds 27 and 28: Ch1, 1sc in next sc, 1sc in each sc to end, join with a sl st.
Round 29: Ch1, sc2tog, [1sc in next sc, sc2tog] to end, join with a sl st. (*20 sts*)
Rounds 30-46: Ch1, 1sc in next sc, 1sc in each sc to end, join with a sl st.
Fasten off.

SNOUT
Round 1: Using two strands of B held together, ch4, join with a sl st to form a ring.
Round 2: Ch1 (counts as first sc), 7sc in ring, join with a sl st. (*8 sts*)
Round 3: Ch1, 2sc in next sc, [1sc in next sc, 2sc in next sc] to end, join with a sl st. (*12 sts*)
Rounds 4 and 5: Ch1, 1sc in next sc, 1sc in each sc to end, join with a sl st.
Round 6: Ch1, 1sc in next sc, 2sc in next sc, [1sc in each of next 2 sc, 2sc in next sc] to end, join with a sl st. (*16 sts*)
Fasten off.

EYE POST COVER
To cover backs of both eyes inside cover.
Row 1: Using two strands of A held together, ch13.
Row 2: 1sc in 2nd ch from hook (missed ch does not count as sc), 1sc in each ch to end. (*12 sts*)
Rows 3 and 4: Ch1 (counts as first sc), 1sc in next sc, 1sc in each sc to end.
Fasten off, leaving a length of yarn.

jack russell golf club cover

Row 10: Ch1, 1sc in same sc, 1sc in each sc to end. (*9 sts*)
Row 11: Ch1, 1sc in same sc, 1sc in each sc to end. (*10 sts*)
Row 12: Sc2tog, 1sc in each sc to last 2 sc, sc2tog. (*8 sts*)
Fasten off.

COLLAR
Row 1: Using C, ch26.
Row 2: 1sc in 2nd ch from hook (missed ch does not count as sc), 1sc in each ch to end. (*25 sts*)
Row 3: Ch1 (counts as first sc), 1sc in next sc, 1sc in each sc to end.
Fasten off.

TO MAKE UP
Before making up it may be advisable to stuff the cover to give the right shape to work with.

Using D, embroider the mouth markings onto the snout (see page 141). Insert the safety nose and secure with the back (see page 141). Stuff the snout firmly and then sew to the head using the photo as a guide. Sew the forehead stripe vertically above the snout.

Attach the safety eyes and then clip off the surplus eye posts. Sew the eye post cover over the eye posts on the inside of the cover.

Sew the ears to the top of the head and then sew collar around the neck.

Add any optional embellishments.

FOREHEAD STRIPE
Row 1: Using two strands of B held together, ch12.
Row 2: 1sc in 2nd ch from hook (missed ch does not count as sc), 1sc in each ch to end. (*11 sts*)
Row 3: Ch1 (counts as first sc), 1sc in next sc, 1sc in each sc to end.
Fasten off.

EARS
(make 2)
Row 1: Using two strands of A held together, ch2.
Row 2: 1sc in 2nd ch from hook (missed ch does not count as sc). (*1 st*)
Row 3: Ch1 (counts as first sc), 1sc in same sc. (*2 sts*)
Row 4: Ch1, 1sc in same sc, 1sc in each sc to end. (*3 sts*)
Row 5: Ch1, 1sc in same sc, 1sc in each sc to end. (*4 sts*)
Row 6: Ch1, 1sc in same sc, 1sc in each sc to end. (*5 sts*)
Row 7: Ch1, 1sc in same sc, 1sc in each sc to end. (*6 sts*)
Row 8: Ch1, 1sc in same sc, 1sc in each sc to end. (*7 sts*)
Row 9: Ch1, 1sc in same sc, 1sc in each sc to end. (*8 sts*)

This little shoulder bag is the ideal size to hold a few essentials. Worked in super bulky yarn for stability, this little bag can carry a coin purse or cell phone and has a snap fastener at the top for security.

husky small shoulder bag

SKILL RATING ● ● ○

YARN AND MATERIALS
King Cole Big Value Super Chunky (100% acrylic), super bulky (super chunky) weight yarn, 90yd (81m) per 3½oz (100g) ball
- 2 balls of Gray 24 (A)
- ½ ball of White 1758 (B)

Small amount of black light worsted (DK) weight yarn (C)

1in (24mm) safety nose

Small amount of toy fiberfill

Pair of ¾in (18mm) safety eyes

⅝in (15mm) snap fastening

Hairspray (optional)

HOOK AND EQUIPMENT
US I-9 (5.5mm) crochet hook

Stitch marker

Yarn needle

Stiff brush or pet brush

FINISHED SIZE
Approx. 6in (15.5cm) square

ABBREVIATIONS
See page 142.

husky small shoulder bag 123

BAG FRONT AND BACK
(make 2)
Row 1: Using A, ch25.
Row 2: 1dc in 3rd ch chain from hook (missed 2 ch do not count as dc), 1dc in each ch to end. (23 sts)
Row 3: Ch3 (counts as first dc), [1FPdc in next dc, 1BPdc in next dc] to last 2 dc, 1FPdc in next dc, 1dc in last dc.
Row 4: Ch3, [1BPdc in next dc, 1FPdc in next dc] to last 2 dc, 1BPdc in next dc, 1dc in last dc.
Repeat Rows 3 and 4 until work measures approx. 6in (15.5cm).
Fasten off.

SNOUT
Round 1: Using B, ch4, join with a sl st to form a ring.
Round 2: Ch1 (counts as first sc), 7sc in ring, join with a sl st. (8 sts)
Round 3: Ch1, 1sc in next sc, 1sc in each sc to end, join with a sl st.
Round 4: Ch1, 2sc in next sc, [1sc in next sc, 2sc in next sc] to end, join with a sl st. (12 sts)
Round 5: Ch1, 1sc in next sc, 1sc in each sc to end, join with a sl st.
Round 6: Ch1, 1sc in next sc, 2sc in next sc, [1sc in each of next 2 sc, 2sc in next sc] to end, join with a sl st. (16 sts)

Rounds 7 and 8: Ch1, 1sc in next sc, 1sc in each sc to end, join with a sl st.
Fasten off.

INNER EARS
(make 2)
Row 1: Using B, ch2.
Row 2: 1sc in 2nd ch from hook (missed ch does not count as sc). (1 st)
Row 3: Ch1 (counts as first sc), 1sc in same st. (2 sts)
Row 4: Ch1, 1sc in same st, 1sc in each sc to end. (3 sts)
Row 5: Ch1, 1sc in same st, 1sc in each sc to end. (4 sts)
Row 6: Ch1, 1sc in same st, 1sc in each sc to end. (5 sts)
Fasten off.

OUTER EARS
(make 2)
Row 1: Using A, ch2.
Row 2: 1sc in 2nd ch from hook (missed ch does not count as sc). (1 st)
Row 3: Ch1 (counts as first sc), 1sc in same st. (2 sts)
Row 4: Ch1, 1sc in same st, 1sc in each sc to end. (3 sts)
Row 5: Ch1, 1sc in same st, 1sc in each sc to end. (4 sts)
Row 6: Ch1, 1sc in same st, 1sc in each sc to end. (5 sts)
Fasten off.

EYE POST COVER
To cover backs of both eyes inside bag.
Row 1: Using A, ch10.
Row 2: 1sc in 2nd ch from hook (missed ch does not count as sc), 1sc in each ch to end. (*9 sts*)
Rows 3 and 4: Ch1 (counts as first sc), 1sc in each sc to end.
Fasten off, leaving a length of yarn for sewing to inside of bag.

SHOULDER STRAP
Row 1: Using A, ch5.
Row 2: 1sc in 2nd ch from hook (missed ch does not count as sc), 1sc in each ch to end. (*4 sts*)
Rows 3-80: Ch1 (counts as first sc), 1sc in next sc, 1sc in each sc to end.
Fasten off.
For a longer strap add more rows if required.

TO MAKE UP
Place the front and back with right sides together. Using A, work a single crochet seam (see page 140) around the sides and bottom, leaving the top edge open. Turn right side out.

Using C, sew long stitches for the mouth onto the snout (see page 141) using the photo as a guide. Insert the safety nose using the photo as a guide and secure with the back (see page 141). Stuff the snout and sew to the front of the bag using the photo as a guide for position.

Add the safety eyes above the snout and secure with the backs. Clip off the surplus eye posts and sew the cover on the inside of the bag to cover the posts.

Place an inner ear piece on top of an outer ear piece, with wrong sides together. Using A, work one round of single crochet evenly around outer edge, working through both layers to join both pieces together and working 2sc in same place at top corner. Sew the ears on either side at the top of the head.

ADDING FUR
Adding the fur on the face can be done in two ways, either with a crochet hook (see page 141) or threading each strand through with a yarn needle and then tying the ends in a knot close to the fabric. The needle is better for getting in small areas, such as around the eyes.

Snout
Cut lengths of B approx. 5in (12.5cm) long. Starting at the side of the snout work lines of fur fringing all around the snout.

Face
Cut lengths of A and continue to add lines of fur fringing around the face approx. 1in (2.5cm) apart until you have covered the full face. Brush with a stiff brush or pet brush to give the fluffy look. Trim to length required.

Fold the strap in half and sew to create a sturdier shoulder strap. Sew the ends of the strap to the top of the bag on either side. Sew in any loose ends (see page 139).

It may be beneficial to spray with hair spray to keep the fur in place (optional).

pug makeup bag

This charming little bag would make a perfect gift for any pug lover. Worked throughout in simple single crochet stitch, this would also look good as a clutch bag—or with a strap added could transform into a small shoulder bag.

SKILL RATING ● ○ ○

YARN AND MATERIALS
King Cole Big Value Super Chunky (100% acrylic), super bulky (super chunky) weight yarn, 90yd (81m) per 3½oz (100g) ball
- 2 balls of Oatmeal 14 (A)
- ½ ball of Black 8 (B)

Small amount of gray light worsted (DK) weight yarn (C)

1in (24mm) safety nose

Small amount of toy fiberfill

Pair of ⅞in (22mm) safety eyes

8in (20cm) zipper fastener

HOOK AND EQUIPMENT
US J-10 (6mm) crochet hook
Stitch marker
Yarn needle
Pins
Sewing needle and thread

FINISHED SIZE
8 x 6½in (20 x 16.5cm)

ABBREVIATIONS
See page 142.

MAKEUP BAG
Row 1: Using A, ch23.
Row 2: 1sc in 2nd ch from hook (missed ch does not count as sc), 1sc in each ch to end. (*22 sts*)
Rows 3–40: Ch1 (counts as first sc), 1sc in next sc, 1sc in each sc to end.
Fasten off.

EYE SURROUNDS
(make 2)
Round 1: Using B, ch4, join with a sl st to form a ring.
Round 2: Ch1 (counts as first sc), 7sc in ring, join with a sl st. (*8 sts*)
Fasten off.

SNOUT
Round 1: Using B, ch9.
Round 2: 1sc in 2nd ch from hook (missed ch counts as first sc), 1sc in each ch to last ch, 3sc in last ch, continuing along other side of chain, 1sc in each ch to missed ch from beginning of round, join with a sl st in missed ch. (*18 sts*)
Round 3: Ch1 (counts as first sc), 1sc in same sc, 1sc in each of next 8 sc, 2sc in next sc, 1sc in each sc to end, join with a sl st. (*20 sts*)
Rounds 4-6: Ch1, 1sc in next sc, 1sc in each sc to end, join with a sl st.
Fasten off.

pug makeup bag 127

EARS
(make 2)
Row 1: Using B, ch2.
Row 2: 1sc in 2nd ch from hook (missed ch does not count as sc). (*1 st*)
Row 3: Ch1 (counts as first sc), 1sc in same sc. (*2 sts*)
Row 4: Ch1, 1sc in same sc, 1sc in each sc to end. (*3 sts*)
Row 5: Ch1, 1sc in same sc, 1sc in each sc to end. (*4 sts*)
Row 6: Ch1, 1sc in next sc, 1sc in each sc to end.
Row 7: Ch1, 1sc in same sc, 1sc in each sc to end. (*5 sts*)
Row 8: Ch1, 1sc in same sc, 1sc in each sc to end. (*6 sts*)
Row 9: Ch1, 1sc in same sc, 1sc in each sc to end. (*7 sts*)
Row 10: Ch1, 1sc in same sc, 1sc in each sc to end. (*8 sts*)
Row 11: Ch1, 1sc in same sc, 1sc in each sc to end. (*9 sts*)
Row 12: Sc2tog, 1sc in each sc to last 2 sc, sc2tog. (*7 sts*)
Fasten off.

TO MAKE UP
Fold the main bag in half with right sides together. Using A, work a single crochet seam (see page 140) along each side edge, leaving the top edge open. Turn right side out.

Using C sew long stitches for the mouth onto the snout (see page 141), using the photo as a guide. Add the safety nose and secure with the back (see page 141). Stuff the snout and sew to the center front of the bag.

Add each eye to an eye surround. Clip off the surplus eye posts, then sew the eyes above the snout using the photo as a guide for position.

Sew the ears to the bag on each top corner at the front.

Pin the zipper in place along the top edges of the bag and then sew in position using the needle and thread.

128 bags and accessories

What a pretty bag, which will be the envy of all Schnauzer lovers! Easy to crochet and worked in super bulky yarn throughout, this bag can be personalized by adding fur in any shade to suit the colors desired.

schnauzer purse

SKILL RATING ● ● ○

YARN AND MATERIALS
King Cole Big Value Super Chunky (100% acrylic), super bulky (super chunky) weight yarn, 90yd (81m) per 3½oz (100g) ball
- 3 balls of Gray 24 (A)
- Small amount of Champagne 12 (white) (B)

Small amount of black light worsted (DK) weight yarn (C)
1³⁄₁₆in (30mm) safety nose
Small amount of toy fiberfill
Pair of 1in (24mm) safety eyes
Pair of bag handles

HOOK AND EQUIPMENT
US J-10 (6mm) crochet hook
Stitch marker
Yarn needle
Stiff brush or pet brush

FINISHED SIZE
Approx. 10 x 10in (25.5 x 25.5cm)

ABBREVIATIONS
See page 142.

BAG FRONT AND BACK
(make 2)
Row 1: Using A, ch33.
Row 2: 1dc in 3rd ch from hook (missed 2 ch do not count as dc), 1dc in each ch to end. (*31 sts*)
Row 3: Ch3 (counts as first dc), [1FPdc in next dc, 1BPdc in next dc] to last 2 dc, 1FPdc in next dc, 1dc in last dc.
Row 4: Ch3, [1BPdc in next dc, 1FPdc in next dc] to last 2 dc, 1BPdc in next dc, 1dc in last dc.
Repeat Rows 3 and 4 until work measures approx. 10in (25.5cm).
Fasten off.

SNOUT
Round 1: Using A, ch4, join with a sl st to form a ring.
Round 2: Ch1 (counts as first sc), 7sc in ring, join with a sl st. (*8 sts*)
Round 3: Ch1, 1sc in same sc, [2sc in next sc] to end, join with a sl st. (*16 sts*)
Round 4: Ch1, 2sc in next sc, [1sc in next sc, 2sc in next sc] to end, join with a sl st. (*24 sts*)
Rounds 5–11: Ch1, 1sc in next sc, 1sc in each sc to end, join with a sl st.
Fasten off.

EYE POST COVER
To cover backs of both eyes inside bag.
Row 1: Using A, ch13.
Row 2: 1sc in 2nd ch from hook (missed ch does not count as sc), 1sc in each ch to end. (*12 sts*)
Rows 3 and 4: Ch1 (counts as first sc), 1sc in next sc, 1sc in each sc to end.
Fasten off, leaving length of yarn.

EARS
(make 2)
Row 1: Using A, ch2.
Row 2: 1sc in 2nd ch from hook (missed ch does not count as sc). (*1 st*)
Row 3: Ch1 (counts as first sc), 1sc in same sc. (*2 sts*)
Row 4: Ch1, 1sc in same sc, 1sc in each sc to end. (*3 sts*)
Row 5: Ch1, 1sc in same sc, 1sc in each sc to end. (*4 sts*)
Row 6: Ch1, 1sc in next sc, 1sc in each sc to end.
Row 7: Ch1, 1sc in same sc, 1sc in each sc to end. (*5 sts*)
Row 8: Ch1, 1sc in same sc, 1sc in each sc to end. (*6 sts*)
Row 9: Ch1, 1sc in same sc, 1sc in each sc to end. (*7 sts*)
Row 10: Ch1, 1sc in same sc, 1sc in each sc to end. (*8 sts*)
Row 11: Ch1, 1sc in same sc, 1sc in each sc to end. (*9 sts*)
Rows 12–14: Ch1, 1sc in next sc, 1sc in each sc to end.
Row 15: Sc2tog, 1sc in each sc to last 2 sc, sc2tog. (*7 sts*)
Fasten off.

TO MAKE UP
Place the front and back with right sides together. Using A, work a single crochet seam (see page 140) around the sides and bottom, leaving the top edge open. Turn right side out.

Using C, sew long stitches for the mouth onto the snout (see page 141) using the photo as a guide. Add the safety nose and secure with the back (see page 141). Stuff the snout and sew to the bag using the photo as a guide for position.

Attach the safety eyes above the snout, using the photo as a guide for position, and secure with the backs. Clip off the surplus eye posts and sew the cover for the backs of the eyes onto the inside of the bag to cover the eye posts.

Sew the ears onto the bag at the top right corners.

ADDING FUR
Adding the fur on the face can be done in two ways, either with a crochet hook (see page 141) or threading each strand through with a yarn needle and then tying the ends in a knot close to the fabric. The needle is better for getting in small areas, such as around the eyes.

Eyebrows
Cut lengths of B approx. 5in (12.5cm) long. Starting above the eye make a short length of fur fringing to make the eyebrow. Repeat for the other eyebrow. Brush with a stiff brush or pet brush to give the fluffy look and trim to length required. The eyebrows should be prominent and stand out.

Snout
Cut lengths of A and B approx. 7in (18cm) long. Add lines of fur fringing on both sides of the snout from the back to the tip of the snout, starting with A and changing to B nearer the front of the snout. Brush and trim as required.

Face
On the bag front and under the snout add lines of fur fringe in A approx. 1in (2.5cm) apart. Trim to the length required and brush for the fluffy effect.

Sew the bag handles in position.

schnauzer purse 131

techniques

This section guides you through all the crochet and finishing techniques that you will need to make the projects in this book.

Holding the hook
Pick up your hook as though you are picking up a pen or pencil. Keeping the hook held loosely between your fingers and thumb, turn your hand so that the palm is facing up and the hook is balanced in your hand and resting in the space between your index finger and your thumb.

You can also hold the hook like a knife—this may be easier if you are working with a large hook or with bulky (chunky) yarn. Choose the method that you find most comfortable.

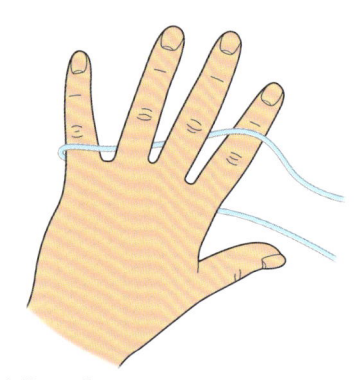

Holding the yarn
1 Pick up the yarn with your little finger in the opposite hand to your hook, with your palm facing upward and with the short end in front. Turn your hand to face downward, with the yarn on top of your index finger and under the other two fingers and wrapped right around the little finger, as shown above.

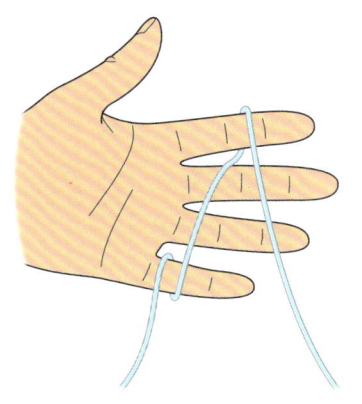

2 Turn your hand to face you, ready to hold the work in your middle finger and thumb. Keeping your index finger only at a slight curve, hold the work or the slip knot using the same hand, between your middle finger and your thumb and just below the crochet hook and loop/s on the hook.

Holding the hook and yarn while crocheting
Keep your index finger, with the yarn draped over it, at a slight curve, and hold your work (or the slip knot) using the same hand, between your middle finger and your thumb and just below the crochet hook and loop/s on the hook.

As you draw the loop through the hook release the yarn on the index finger to allow the loop to stay loose on the hook. If you tense your index finger, the yarn will become too tight and pull the loop on the hook too tight for you to draw the yarn through.

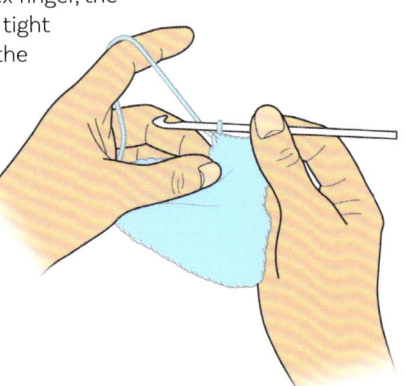

Holding the hook and yarn for left-handers
Some left-handers learn to crochet like right-handers, but others learn with everything reversed—with the hook in the left hand and the yarn in the right.

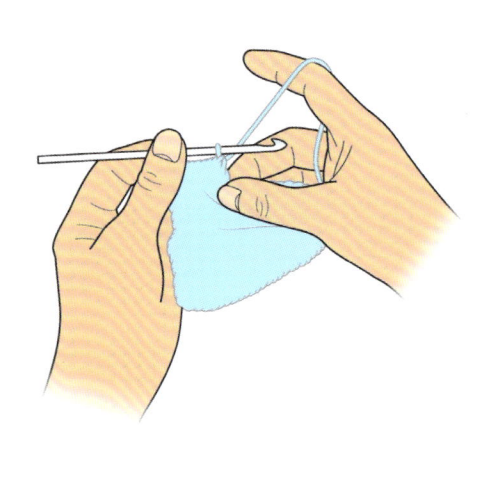

Making a slip knot

The simplest way is to make a circle with the yarn, so that the loop is facing downward.

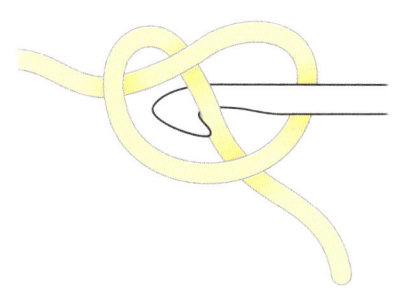

1 In one hand hold the circle at the top where the yarn crosses, and let the tail drop down at the back so that it falls across the center of the loop. With your free hand or the tip of a crochet hook, pull a loop through the circle.

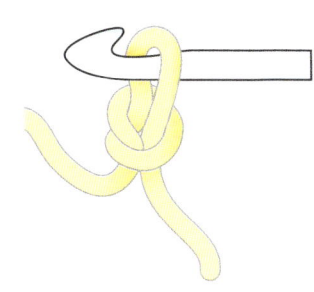

2 Put the hook into the loop and pull gently so that it forms a loose loop on the hook.

Yarn over hook (yoh)

To create a stitch, catch the yarn from behind with the hook pointing upward. As you gently pull the yarn through the loop on the hook, turn the hook so it faces downward and slide the yarn through the loop. The loop on the hook should be kept loose enough for the hook to slide through easily.

Chain (ch)

1 Using the hook, wrap the yarn over the hook ready to pull it through the loop on the hook.

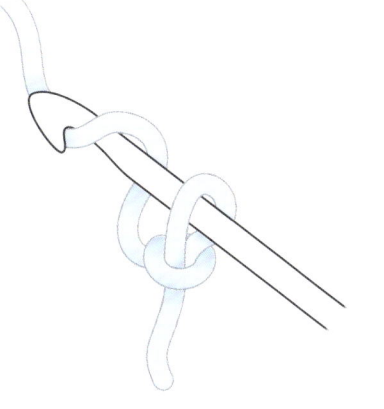

2 Pull through, creating a new loop on the hook. Continue in this way to create a chain of the required length.

Chain ring

If you are crocheting a round shape, one way of starting off is by crocheting a number of chains following the instructions in your pattern, and then joining them into a circle.

1 To join the chain into a circle, insert the crochet hook into the first chain that you made (not into the slip knot), yarn over hook.

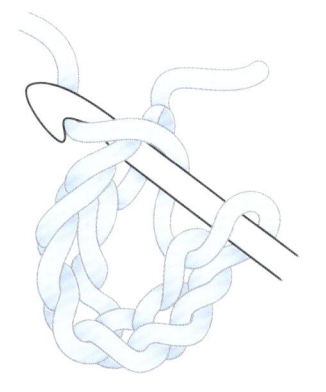

2 Pull the yarn through the chain and through the loop on your hook at the same time, thereby creating a slip stitch and forming a circle. You now have a chain ring ready to work stitches into as instructed in the pattern.

techniques 133

Slip stitch (sl st)

A slip stitch doesn't create any height and is often used as the last stitch to create a smooth and even round or row.

1 To make a slip stitch: first put the hook through the work, yarn over hook.

2 Pull the yarn through both the work and through the loop on the hook at the same time, so you will have 1 loop on the hook.

Making rounds

When working in rounds the work is not turned, so you are always working from one side. Depending on the pattern you are working, a "round" can be square. Start each round by making one or more chains to create the height you need for the stitch you are working:

Single crochet = 1 chain
Half double crochet = 2 chains
Double crochet = 3 chains
Treble crochet = 4 chains

Work the required stitches to complete the round. At the end of the round, slip stitch into the top of the chain to close the round.

Continuous spiral

If you work in a spiral you do not need a turning chain. After completing the base ring, place a stitch marker in the first stitch and then continue to crochet around. When you have made a round and reached the point where the stitch marker is, work this stitch, take out the stitch marker from the previous round and put it back into the first stitch of the new round. A safety pin or piece of yarn in a contrasting color makes a good stitch marker.

Making rows

When making straight rows you turn the work at the end of each row and make a turning chain to create the height you need for the stitch you are working with, as for making rounds.

Single crochet = 1 chain
Half double crochet = 2 chains
Double crochet = 3 chains
Treble crochet = 4 chains

Working into top of stitch

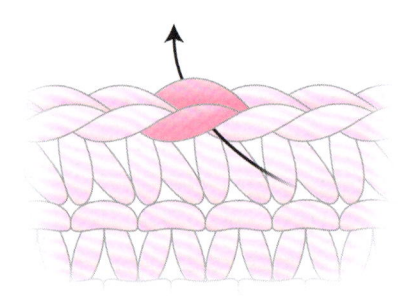

Unless otherwise directed, always insert the hook under both of the two loops on top of the stitch—this is the standard technique.

Working into front loop of stitch (FLO)

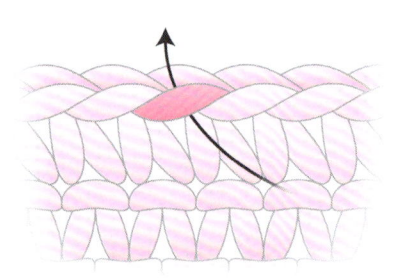

To work into the front loop of a stitch, pick up the front loop from underneath at the front of the work.

Working into back loop of stitch (BLO)

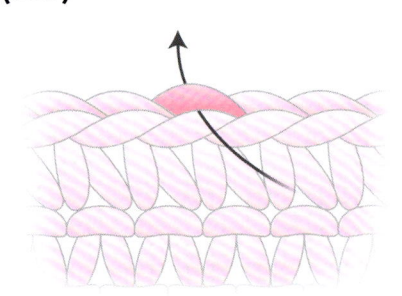

To work into the back loop of the stitch, insert the hook between the front and the back loop, picking up the back loop from the front of the work.

Working around the front or back post

Stitches can also be worked around the "posts"—or "stems"—of the stitches in the previous row/round. These steps show how to work a double crochet stitch around to the front and the back of the post, but the same principle applies to other stitches worked around the back. They can be used to create texture.

Raised double crochet round front

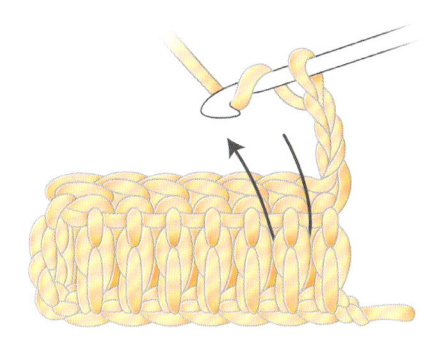

1 Yarn over hook and insert the hook from the front and around the post (the stem) of the next double crochet from right to left.

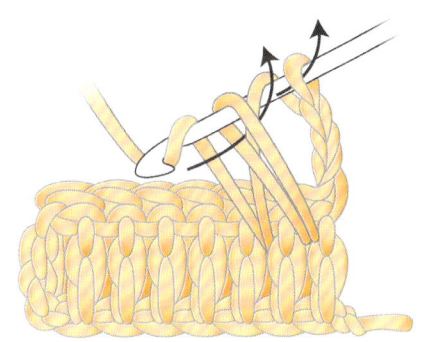

2 Yarn over hook and pull the yarn through the work, yarn over hook, and pull the yarn through the first 2 loops on the hook.

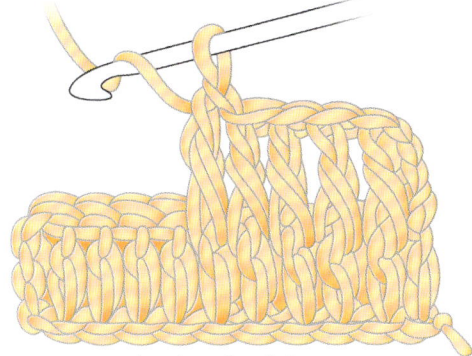

3 Yarn over hook and pull the yarn through the 2 loops on the hook (1 loop on the hook).

Raised double crochet round back

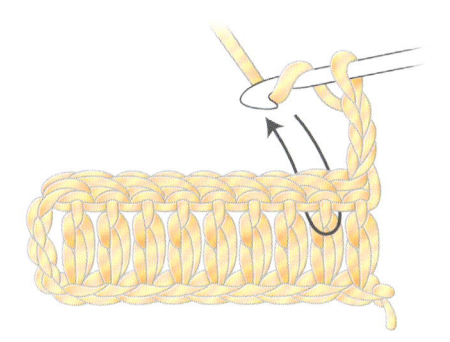

1 Yarn over hook and insert the hook from the back and around the post (the stem) of the next double crochet as directed in the pattern from right to left.

2 Yarn over hook and pull the yarn through the work, yarn over hook, and pull the yarn through the first 2 loops on the hook.

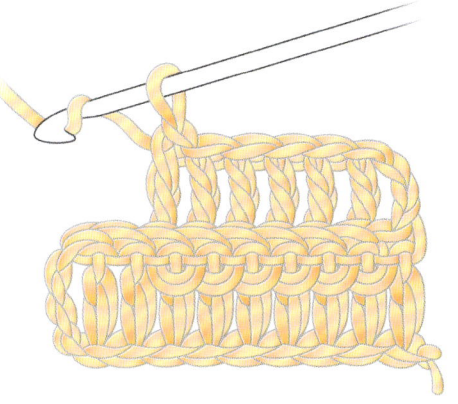

3 Yarn over hook and pull the yarn through the 2 loops on the hook (1 loop on the hook).

techniques

Single crochet (sc)

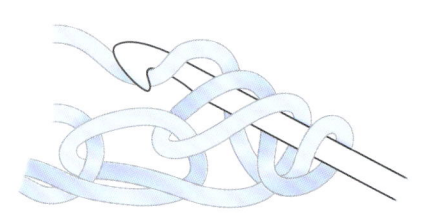

1 Insert the hook into your work, yarn over hook, and pull the yarn through the work only. You will then have 2 loops on the hook.

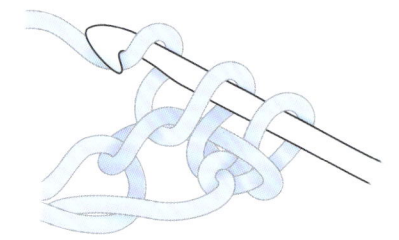

2 Yarn over hook again and pull through the 2 loops on the hook. You will then have 1 loop on the hook.

Half double crochet (hdc)

1 Before inserting the hook into the work, wrap the yarn over the hook and put the hook through the work with the yarn wrapped around.

2 Yarn over hook again and pull through the first loop on the hook. You now have 3 loops on the hook.

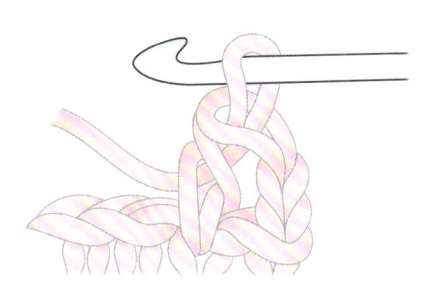

3 Yarn over hook and pull the yarn through all 3 loops. You will be left with 1 loop on the hook.

Double crochet (dc)

1 Before inserting the hook into the work, wrap the yarn over the hook. Put the hook through the work with the yarn wrapped around, yarn over hook again, and pull through the first loop on the hook. You now have 3 loops on the hook.

2 Yarn over hook again, pull the yarn through the first 2 loops on the hook. You now have 2 loops on the hook.

3 Pull the yarn through 2 loops again. You will be left with 1 loop on the hook.

Increasing

Make two or three stitches into one stitch or space from the previous row. The illustration shows a double crochet increase being made.

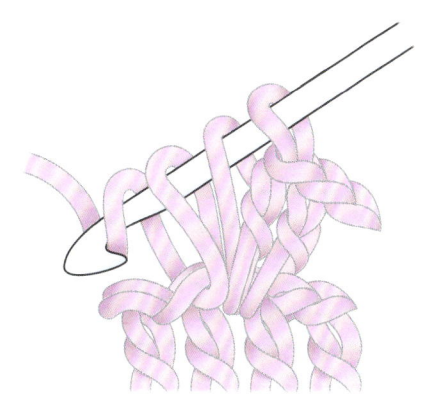

Decreasing

You can decrease by either missing the next stitch and continuing to crochet, or by crocheting two or more stitches together. The basic technique for crocheting stitches together is the same, no matter which stitch you are using. The following example shows sc2tog.

Single crochet two stitches together (sc2tog)

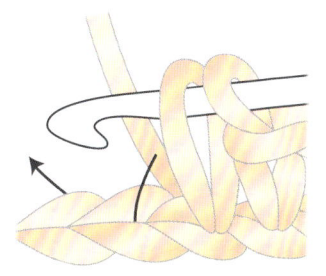

1 Insert the hook into your work, yarn over hook, and pull the yarn through the work (2 loops on hook). Insert the hook in next stitch, yarn over hook, and pull the yarn through.

2 Yarn over hook again and pull through all 3 loops on the hook. You will then have 1 loop on the hook.

Joining yarn at the end of a row or round

You can use this technique when changing color, or when joining in a new ball of yarn as one runs out.

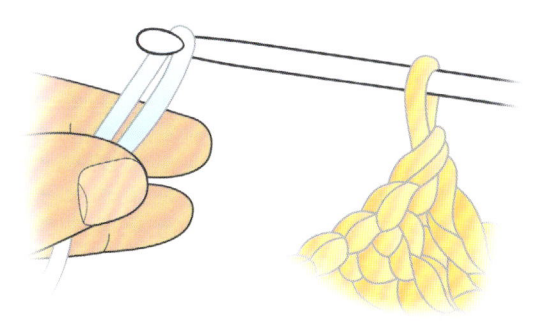

1 Keep the loop of the old yarn on the hook. Drop the tail and catch a loop of the strand of the new yarn with the crochet hook.

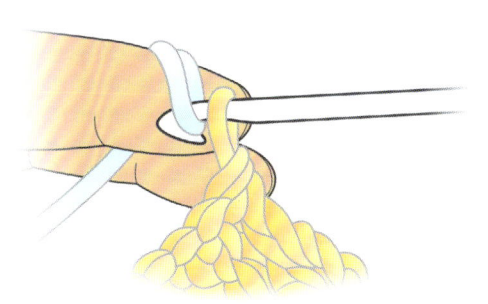

2 Draw the new yarn through the loop on the hook, keeping the old loop drawn tight and continue as instructed in the pattern.

techniques

Joining in new yarn after fastening off

1 Fasten off the old color (see opposite). Make a slip knot with the new color (see page 133). Insert the hook into the stitch at the beginning of the next row, then through the slip knot.

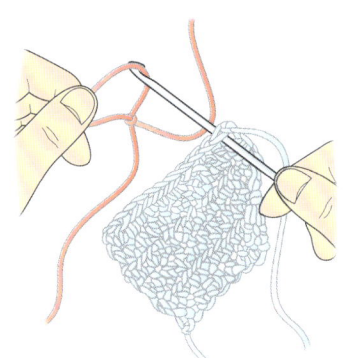

2 Draw the loop of the slip knot through to the front of the work. Carry on working using the new color, following the instructions in the pattern.

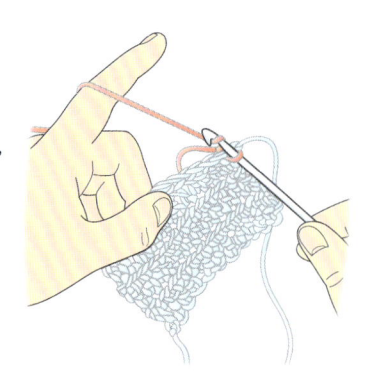

Joining yarn in the middle of a row or round
For a neat color join in the middle of a row or round, use these methods.

Joining a new color into single crochet

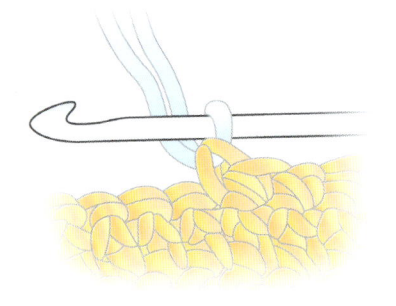

1 Make a single crochet stitch (see page 136), but do not draw the final loop through, so there are 2 loops on the hook. Drop the old yarn, catch the new yarn with the hook, and draw it through both loops to complete the stitch and join in the new color at the same time.

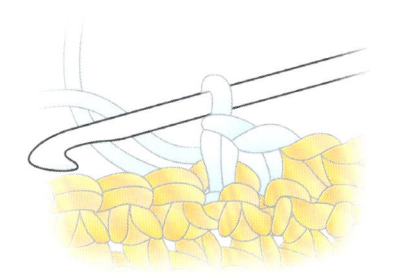

2 Continue to crochet with the new yarn. Cut the old yarn leaving a 6in (15cm) tail and weave the tail in (see right) after working a row, or once the work is complete.

Joining a new color into double crochet

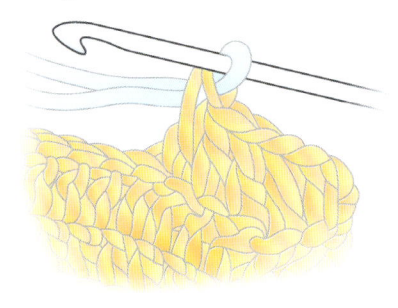

1 Make a double crochet stitch (see page 136), but do not draw the final loop through, so there are 2 loops on the hook. Drop the old yarn, catch the new yarn with the hook, and draw it through both loops to complete the stitch and join in the new color at the same time.

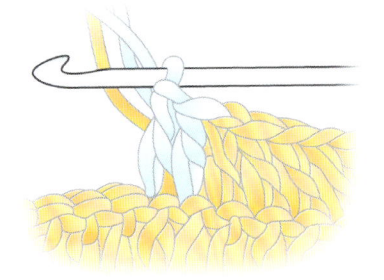

2 Continue to crochet with the new yarn. Cut the old yarn leaving a 6in (15cm) tail and sew the tail in (see right) after working a row, or once the work is complete.

Enclosing a yarn tail

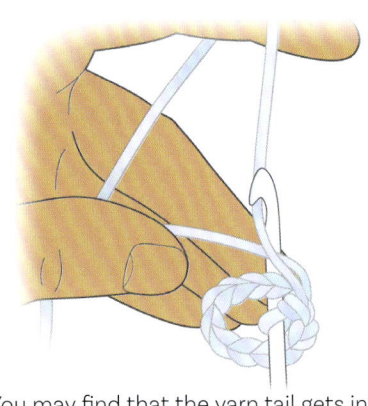

You may find that the yarn tail gets in the way as you work; you can enclose this into the stitches as you go by placing the tail at the back as you wrap the yarn. This also saves having to sew this tail end in later.

Fastening off

When you have finished crocheting, you need to fasten off the stitches to stop all your work unraveling.

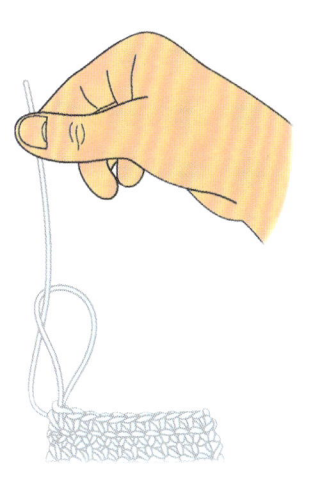

Draw up the final loop of the last stitch to make it bigger. Cut the yarn, leaving a tail of approximately 4in (10cm)—unless a longer end is needed for sewing up. Pull the tail all the way through the loop and pull the loop up tightly.

Sewing in yarn ends

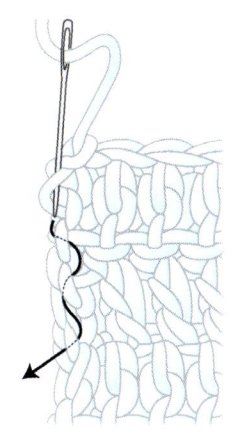

It is important to sew in the tail ends of the yarn so that they are secure and your crochet won't unravel. Thread a yarn needle with the tail end of yarn. On the wrong side, take the needle through the crochet one stitch down on the edge, then take it through the stitches, working in a gentle zig-zag. Work through four or five stitches then return in the opposite direction. Remove the needle, pull the crochet gently to stretch it, and trim the end.

Blocking

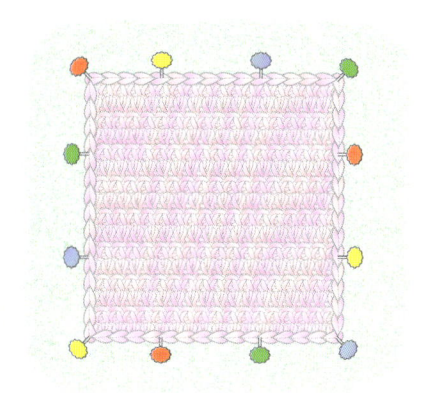

Crochet can tend to curl, so to make flat pieces stay flat you may need to block them. Pin the piece out to the correct size and shape on an ironing board or some soft foam mats (such as the ones sold as children's play mats). Spray the crochet with water and leave it to dry completely before unpinning and removing from the board or mats.

Making an oversewn seam

An oversewn join gives a nice flat seam and is the simplest and most common joining technique.

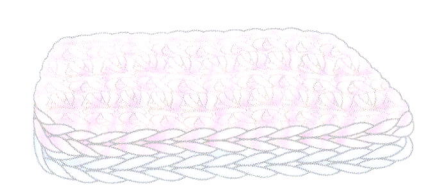

1 Thread a yarn sewing needle with the yarn you're using in the project. Place the pieces to be joined with right sides together.

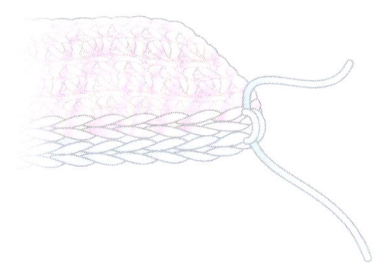

2 Insert the needle in one corner in the top loops of the stitches of both pieces and pull up the yarn, leaving a tail of about 2in (5cm). Go into the same place with the needle and pull up the yarn again; repeat two or three times to secure the yarn at the start of the seam.

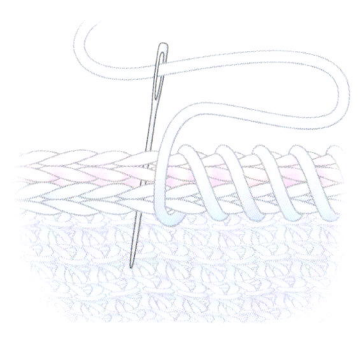

3 Join the pieces together by taking the needle through the loops at the top of corresponding stitches on each piece to the end. Fasten off the yarn at the end, as in step 2.

techniques 139

Making a single crochet seam or slip stitch seam

With a single crochet seam you join two pieces together using a crochet hook and working a single crochet stitch through both pieces, instead of sewing them together with a tail of yarn and a yarn sewing needle. This makes a quick and strong seam and gives a slightly raised finish to the edging. For a less raised seam, follow the same basic technique, but work each stitch in slip stitch rather than single crochet.

1 Start by lining up the two pieces with wrong sides together. Insert the hook in the top 2 loops of the stitch of the first piece, then into the corresponding stitch on the second piece.

2 Complete the single crochet stitch as normal and continue on the next stitches as directed in the pattern. This gives a raised effect if the single crochet stitches are made on the right side of the work.

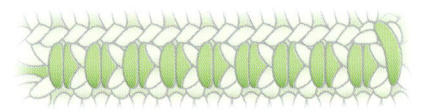

3 You can work with the wrong side of the work facing (with the pieces right side facing) if you don't want this effect and it still creates a good strong join.

Surface crochet

Surface crochet is a simple way to add extra decoration to a finished item, working slip stitches over the surface of the fabric.

1 Using a contrast yarn, make a slip knot (see page 133). Holding the yarn with the slip knot behind the work and the hook in front, insert the hook between two stitches from front to the back and catch the slip knot behind the work with the hook. Draw the slip knot back through, so there is 1 loop on the hook at the front of the work.

2 Insert the hook between the next 2 stitches, yarn over hook and draw a loop through to the front. You will now have 2 loops on the hook.

3 Pull the first loop on the hook through the second loop to complete the first slip stitch on the surface of the work. Repeat steps 2 and 3 to make the next slip stitch. To join two ends with an invisible join, cut the yarn and thread onto a yarn needle. Insert the needle up through the last stitch, into the first stitch as if you were crocheting it, then into the back loop of the previous stitch. Fasten off on the wrong side.

Embroidery

These decorative hand-sewing techniques are used to add mouths, eyes, and noses to some of the projects.

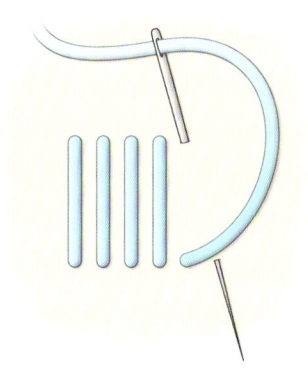

Straight stitch
Bring the needle through to the surface of the fabric and then take it back down to create a small straight stitch. These can be worked as part of a mouth design.

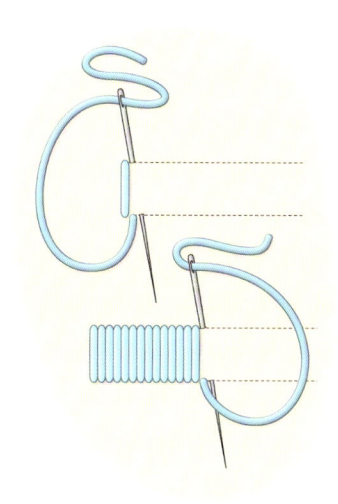

Satin stitch
Bring the needle up to the surface of the fabric, then take it back down at the selected point, drawing the yarn flush against the fabric. Bring the needle back up and down again next to the previous stitch. Continue in this manner, drawing the yarn smoothly against the surface of the fabric to fill the chosen area. The stitches should be close together, with no fabric visible in between them. They can be worked to create eyes or a nose on your finished crocheted dog project.

Adding safety eyes/noses

Note: If you're making a project for a young child, instead of adding a safety nose and eyes, embroider these features using straight stitch and satin stitch (see above).

Insert each eye from the front and make sure both eyes are completely level and sitting on the same round before you secure the safety catches at the back. The flat piece of the safety catch is pushed toward the crochet piece from the inside. Use the same method to insert the safety nose.

A safety eye insertion tool will make fitting the eyes easier. This usually consists of a piece of metal or plastic with holes for extra leverage when securing the eye washers.

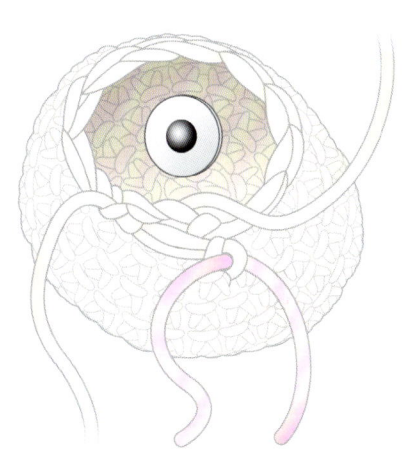

Adding fur

Adding the fur on the face can be done in two ways, either with a crochet hook or threading each strand through with a yarn needle and then tying the ends into a knot close to the fabric. The needle is better for getting into small areas, such as around the eyes.

To add a piece of "fur" using a crochet hook, take two strands of yarn and fold them in half. Insert the crochet hook in the first stitch and hook the folded yarn loop. Pull the loop through about a third of the way. Now open up the loop (both pieces of yarn) and slip the ends of the yarn (all 4 ends) through the loop. Gently pull it tight to create the first piece of fringe. You may need to adjust the ends as you tighten to get them all even.

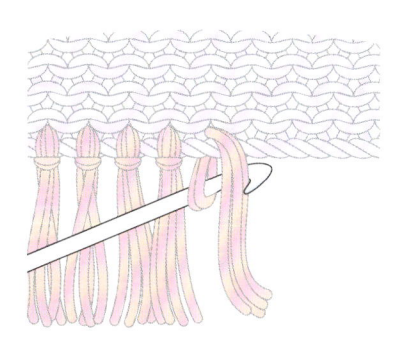

Abbreviations

Approx.	approximately
BP	work stitch around post of next stitch from back to front
BLO	work in the back loop only
ch	chain
cont	continue
dc	double crochet
FLO	work in the front loop only
FP	work stitch around post of next stitch from front to back
hdc	half double crochet
sc	single crochet
sc2tog	single crochet next two stitches together
sl st	slip stitch
st(s)	stitch(es)
[ ]	work stitches inside square brackets the number of times stated

Special abbreviations

FPdc (front post double crochet): a double crochet worked by inserting your hook around the post of the next stitch from front to back to front, rather than into the top two loops of a stitch as you normally would.

BPdc (back post double crochet): a double crochet worked by inserting your hook around the post of the next stitch from back to front to back, rather than into the top two loops of a stitch as you normally would.

....

Crochet stitch conversion chart

Crochet stitches are worked in the same way in both the USA and the UK, but the stitch names are not the same and identical names are used for different stitches. Below is a list of the UK terms used in this book, and the equivalent US terms.

US TERM	UK TERM
single crochet (sc)	double crochet (dc)
half double crochet (hdc)	half treble (htr)
double crochet (dc)	treble (tr)
gauge	tension
yarn over hook (yoh)	yarn round hook (yrh)

142 techniques

index

abbreviations 141

bags
   Chocolate Labrador Makeup Bag and Coin Purses 116-19
   Cockapoo Purse 110-12
   Husky Shoulder Bag 123-5
   Labradoodle Clutch Bag 104-6
   Maltese Terrier Purses 107-9
   Pug Makeup Bag 126-8
   Schnauzer Purse 129-31
   Shih Tzu Purse 98-100
   Terrier Tote Bag 101-3
Bearded Collie Pillow 19-21
Bichon Frise Pillow 37-9
blocking 139
Border Collie Pillow 34-6
Brown Spaniel Pillow 28-30

Cairn Terrier 74-8
chain stitch 133
Chihuahua Nutcracker 79-83
Chocolate Labrador Pillow 43-5
Chocolate Labrador Makeup Bag and Coin Purses 116-19
Cockapoo Purse 110-12
conversion charts 141
crochet techniques 132-40

Dachshund Draft Excluder 54-8
decreasing 137
doorstops, Poodle 62-5
double crochet 136
draft excluder Dachshund 54-8

embroidery 141
eyes, adding 141

fastening off 139
Fluffy Dog Silhouette Pillows 25-7
Framed Fluffy Dog Wall Hanging 66-8
Framed Poodles 69-71
French Bulldog Pillow 46-8
fur, adding 141

German Shepherd Pillow 40-2
golf club covers
   Jack Russell Terrier 120-2
   Poodle 113-15

half double crochet 136
hook, holding 133
Husky Pillow 13-15
Husky Shoulder Bag 123-5

increasing 137

Jack Russell Terrier Golf Club Cover 120-2

Labradoodle Clutch Bag 104-6

Maltese Terrier Purses 107-9

noses, adding 141

Old English Sheepdog Pillow 10-12
oversewn seams 139

pillows
   Bearded Collie 19-21
   Bichon Frise 37-9
   Border Collie 34-6
   Brown Spaniel 28-30
   Chocolate Labrador 43-5
   Fluffy Dog Silhouette 25-7
   French Bulldog 46-8
   German Shepherd 40-2
   Husky 13-15
   Old English Sheepdog 10-12
   Poodle 49-51
   Terrier Square 31-3
   West Highland Terrier 16-18
   Yorkshire Terrier 22-4
Pomeranian Halloween Pal 88-91
Poodle Pillow 49-51
Poodle Doorstops 62-5
Poodle Golf Club Covers 113-15
Poodles, Framed 69-71
Pug Makeup Bag 126-8
puppies: Dachshund Draft Excluder 54-8

raised double crochet round front or back 135
rounds 134
rows 134

Schnauzer Purse 129-31
seams 139-40
Shih Tzu Purse 98-100
single crochet 136
single crochet seam 140
slip knots 133
slip stitch 134
slip stitch seam 140
Spaniel Cuddle Buddy 84-7
surface crochet 140

techniques 132-41
Terrier Square Pillow 31-3
Terrier Tote Bag 101-3

wall hanging: Framed Fluffy Dog 66-8
weaving in 139
West Highland Terrier Cuddle Pal 92-5
West Highland Terrier Pillow 16-18

yarn
   enclosing tails 138
   holding 132
   joining 137-8
Yorkshire Terrier 74-8
Yorkshire Terrier Pillow 22-4

Suppliers

We cannot cover all stockists here, so please explore the local yarn stores and online retailers in your own country. If you wish to substitute a different yarn for the one recommended in the pattern, try the Yarnsub website for suggestions: www.yarnsub.com.

King Cole yarns
www.kingcole.com

USA
LoveCrafts
Online sales
www.lovecrafts.com

Knitting Fever Inc.
www.knittingfever.com

WEBS
www.yarn.com

Jo-Ann Fabric and Craft Stores
Yarns and craft supplies
www.joann.com

Michaels
Craft supplies
www.michaels.com

UK
LoveCrafts
Online sales
www.lovecrafts.com

Wool
Yarn, hooks
Store in Bath
+44 (0)1225 469144
www.woolbath.co.uk

Wool Warehouse
Online sales
www.woolwarehouse.co.uk

Laughing Hens
Online sales
Tel: +44 (0) 1829 740903
www.laughinghens.com

John Lewis
Yarns and craft supplies
Telephone numbers of stores on website
www.johnlewis.com

Hobbycraft
Yarns and craft supplies
www.hobbycraft.co.uk

Australia
Black Sheep Wool 'n' Wares
Retail store and online
Tel: +61 (0)2 6779 1196
www.blacksheepwool.com.au

Sun Spun
Retail store (Canterbury, Victoria) and online
Tel: +61 (0)3 9830 1609
www.sunspun.com.au

Acknowledgments

Thank you to the following people for all your help and support to make this book possible:

My husband Stuart and daughter Rebecca.

Susan Mears, my agent.

Joanne Whitehead from King Cole Ltd.